LAND AND SEA:

The Lyric Poetry of Philip Freneau

LAND AND SEA:

The Lyric Poetry
of
Philip Freneau

~~~~~~

By Richard C. Vitzthum

Associate Professor
Department of English Language and Literature
University of Maryland

UNIVERSITY OF MINNESOTA PRESS,

MINNEAPOLIS

Copyright © 1978 by the University of Minnesota.
All rights reserved.
Printed in the United States of America
at the University of Minnesota Printing Department, Minneapolis.
Published by the University of Minnesota Press,
2037 University Avenue Southeast, Minneapolis, Minnesota 55455,
and published in Canada by Burns & MacEachern
Limited, Don Mills, Ontario

The University of Minnesota is an equal opportunity
educator and employer.

Library of Congress Cataloging in Publication Data

Vitzthum, Richard C.   1936-
    Land and sea.

    Includes bibliographical references and index.
    1. Freneau, Philip Morin, 1752-1832 —Criticism and
interpretation. I. Title.
PS759.V5   811'.2   77-93379
ISBN 0-8166-0860-1

Acknowledgments

Among the many scholars whose advice I have profited from while writing this book, I owe special thanks to Lewis Leary of the University of North Carolina, whose suggestions have been unfailingly generous and helpful. I am also indebted to Calhoun Winton and Jackson Bryer of the University of Maryland and to Sargent Bush of the University of Wisconsin, all of whom reviewed the manuscript at one stage or another of its development. In addition, I wish to thank David Levin of the University of Virginia for having introduced me to early American literature many years ago at Stanford. During the past decade, I have learned much about Freneau from several students in my graduate seminar at Maryland and especially from Jeffrey Griffith, whose recent doctoral dissertation sheds valuable light on Freneau's poetry. To my wife, who has helped me type, edit, and proofread from beginning to end, my heartfelt thanks. Finally, I am deeply grateful to the Maryland Research Board for supporting this project financially in 1974 and again in 1977.

College Park, Maryland   Richard C. Vitzthum

Table of Contents

LAND AND SEA:

The Lyric Poetry of Philip Freneau

I

Introduction

In 1929 Harry Hayden Clark concluded that as a poet Philip
Freneau was "unable to select and focus with concentrated in-
tensity truly significant experience in such a way as to stir the
reader's imagination, to suggest a symbolic quality."[1] Most
twentieth-century students have agreed with Clark, treating
Freneau as historically rather than aesthetically important and
focusing more on his biography than on his art. Yet an irony
of this biographical emphasis has been that aside from a handful of letters, some marginalia, a scattering of public records,
and one or two recollections from people who knew him, almost no solid information about Freneau's day-to-day existence has survived. Biographers have had to infer Freneau's
thoughts, feelings, and activities during long periods almost
solely from his published writing. Because they have found little depth or coherence even in his best work, they have drawn a
portrait, based largely on unsympathetic readings of his poetry,
of a well-intentioned but superficial and muddled artist.

The basic biographical facts can be quickly summarized.
Born January 2, 1752, to Pierre Freneau, a New York merchant and son of a Huguenot immigrant, Philip grew up in Mt.

Pleasant, New Jersey, on an estate his mother's family gave the Freneaus shortly before Philip was born. Aiming Philip for the Presbyterian ministry, Pierre sent him in 1763 to school first in New York City and then in Manalapan, New Jersey, to prepare for college. When, broken by sickness and debt, Pierre died in 1767, Philip's mother Agnes decided to carry out the plan. In 1768, through strict economies, she enrolled him at Princeton, then the College of New Jersey, where among his twelve classmates were Hugh Henry Brackenridge and James Madison. Having compiled a respectable record, Freneau graduated in 1771, offering a commencement poem titled "The Rising Glory of America," written in collaboration with Brackenridge, as the capstone of his college career. In 1772 he taught grammar school in Flatbush, Long Island, for a week or two; published a volume of pastoral verse; and joined Brackenridge at Somerset Academy, near Princess Anne, Maryland, as a teacher. In 1773 and 1774 he may have studied theology, possibly with the idea of becoming a minister, but by 1775 he had given it up and found his way to New York, where in the latter half of the year he published a dozen poems attacking the British and their American sympathizers and defending the growing revolution. Then, in early 1776, he left North America for the Caribbean and spent the next two years on commerical or privateering voyages, apparently using as home base the estate of John Hanson, a wealthy slave owner and planter, on the island of Santa Cruz.

Returning to New Jersey in the summer of 1778, he enlisted as a private in the state militia, but for the next two years soldiering seems to have occupied him less than seafaring. In late 1778, for instance, he commanded a cargo ship on a voyage to the Caribbean, a feat that proves how expert a sailor he had become during the two previous years. While publishing prose and poetry in Brackenridge's *United States Magazine* during 1779, he may have supported himself by serving on board ves-

sels sailing out of Philadelphia. Perhaps he was part owner of
the brig *Aurora*, which was captured by the British with him
aboard off the Jersey coast on its maiden voyage from Philadelphia in May 1780. For the next six weeks he was held pris-
oner in New York harbor, first on the prison ship *Scorpion*,
then the hospital ship *Hunter* — an experience that inspired his
poem *The British Prison Ship* and permanently embittered him
against England. In 1781 and 1782 he probably helped Francis
Bailey edit the liberal, anti-British *Freeman's Journal*, certainly
contributing much prose and poetry to it in any case. He also
served as a clerk in the Philadelphia Post Office in 1783 but gave
up that job in 1784 to go to sea again, probably in hopes of
earning enough in the shipping business to marry Eleanor Forman, a neighbor in Mt. Pleasant with whom he seems to have
fallen in love in the early 1780s.

During the next six years Freneau commanded several commercial vessels on the coastal-Caribbean-mid-Atlantic trade
routes, published two book-length collections of his poetry
through Bailey in 1786 and 1788, and doubtless carried on a
social life in the New York-Mt. Pleasant-Philadelphia area and
in Charleston, South Carolina, where his brother Peter was a
leading citizen. But in 1790 he left the ocean to marry Miss
Forman and become editor of the New York *Daily Advertiser*,
a post he gave up in the spring of 1791. At the urging of his
former classmate Madison and with the financial backing of
Secretary of State Thomas Jefferson, Freneau next founded
and edited *The National Gazette* — a newspaper designed to
counteract the Federalist *United States Gazette*, edited by
John Fenno but controlled by Treasury Secretary Alexander
Hamilton. For two years, from October 1791 to October 1793,
he successfully managed this enterprise at the center of national
politics in Philadelphia, helping blunt the Federalists' power
and articulate and promulgate the Jeffersonian policies that
were to be put into practice in 1801. When for financial reasons

beyond his control *The National Gazette* collapsed in 1793, Freneau returned to Mt. Pleasant and established his own press, which published almanacs, a new collection of his poetry (1795), and yet another newspaper, *The Jersey Chronicle*, which existed from May 1795 to April 1796. In 1797 he moved his growing family to New York and founded still another newspaper, *The Time Piece and Literary Companion*, which he edited from March 1797 to March 1798.

For the next three years the record is murky. Although Freneau took several trips to Charleston and published a good deal of prose and poetry—most of it supporting the Jeffersonian cause against John Adams and the Federalists—he seems to have had no fixed source of income other than the Mt. Pleasant farm, parts of which he sold during this period, presumably to help support his wife and four daughters. When the Republicans came to power in 1801, friends solicited a government post for him from Madison and Jefferson, but either he or they refused and nothing came of it. The extent of his financial problems during this period, if in fact he saw them as such, and their effect on him and his family are vague.

Between 1802 and 1807 he returned to the sea and sailed several vessels, apparently as captain, up and down the eastern seaboard and at least twice to Madeira, drawing a number of lyric poems from the experience and, in the breaks between voyages, writing topical pieces as well. In 1807, partly as a result of Jefferson's embargo, he retired permanently from the sea to New Jersey, where he spent the remaining twenty-five years of his life. At the request of Lydia Bailey, a poor relative of his friend and former publisher, he prepared a new collection of his poems in 1809, the proceeds of which he gave her in Francis Bailey's memory. Before and during the War of 1812 he continued writing political and nonpolitical verse and prose, and in 1815 he collected in two new volumes the poetry he had written since 1795 and had not included in the 1809 edition. The old home in Mt. Pleasant burned to the ground in 1818, taking with it virtually all his papers, manuscripts, and correspondence and forcing him to move to another house in the area. Before his death near Freehold, New Jersey, on December 18, 1832, from exposure in a snowstorm, he had sold most of his property and applied for a government pension of thirty-five dollars a year.[2]

Beyond these and a smattering of other factual details lies biographical darkness—save for Freneau's published writing. What sort of man do the 550-odd poems and the scores of prose pieces he published reveal? F. L. Pattee, the first of the modern scholarly biographers, defined him in 1902 as "a man equipped by nature for a true poet, a man with a message, yet dwarfed and transformed by his environment."[3] Arguing that Freneau was a poet fifty years ahead of his time, Pattee pictures him as abandoning his youthful idealism and lyricism in face of the realities of the Revolutionary era, exchanging "his old poetic ideals for those of mere reason and common sense."[4] Pattee admires him for an early poem, "The House of Night," which he sees as a foreshadowing of the gothicism of Coleridge and Poe; for his revolt against the artificialities of eighteenth-century poetic diction in poems like "The Wild Honey-Suckle," with its Wordsworthian celebration of a humble subject; and for his use of American materials in "The Indian Burying-Ground" and similar poems. Had Freneau been a great poet, Pattee contends, he could not only have helped free English poetry from its eighteenth-century shackles but have unequivocally declared America's literary independence of Europe. But he was not a great poet, however talented he may have been, and chose after the American Revolutionary War to slip gradually into what Pattee sees as the comfortable mediocrity of his later verse: "It took twenty-five years to kill the spark in his breast, but the process though slow was sure."[5] The reason for this snuffing out, argues Pattee, was that Freneau's "temperament was Celtic. He inherited with his French blood a passionate love for beauty, a sensuous, dreamy delight in the merely poetic, in the weird and romantic. He had not the Teutonic stability; he was easily exalted, easily depressed; he went often to extremes; he was sensitive to a degree that made criticism a torture, and he was proud beyond all reason."[6] Like a rococo motif in a Victorian salon, this racial characterization crops up again and again in Pattee's sketch: e.g., "A bard with more Teutonic blood . . . would have staid at his post"; or, "His Celtic temperament would not patiently wait for recognition, as did Wordsworth; he was too proud to force his poetry upon an unwilling public."[7]

Pattee's interpretation, its racial corrugations flattened, has dominated Freneau scholarship to the present day. Professor Clark, in the introduction to his 1929 selection of Freneau's poetry, agrees that Freneau's chief poetic contributions were concrete, proto-Wordsworthian images of American nature and that "his genius was thwarted by an age and associates indifferent to 'pure poetry,' believing, in the words of Madison, 'that something more substantial, more durable, more profitable befits our riper age.' "[8] Although Clark stresses the transitional nature of Freneau's poetry more heavily than Pattee, contributing, for instance, the valuable point that Freneau eventually embraced a deism midway between orthodox Christianity and modern agnosticism, he too sees Freneau as having an "aversion to restraint"[9] that resulted in an absence of "focused vision"[10] in his poetry. This lack of restraint, according to Clark, "accounts, also, for his too frequently slipshod metrical and rhyming effects."[11]

In 1941 Lewis Leary etched this interpretive tradition in the granite of his monumental biography, *That Rascal Freneau: A Study in Literary Failure.* Opening his book with the statement that "Philip Freneau failed in almost everything he attempted,"[12] Leary goes on to present every piece of evidence that suggested Freneau's impulsiveness, his sensuousness as opposed to rationality, and his inability to deal with the practical world, and weaves it together as a chronicle of financial, intellectual, and literary defeat. Dismissing study of "the philosophical basis of Freneau's writings" as "an unprofitable occupation,"[13] Leary, like Pattee and Clark, argues that Freneau was "a poet whose mind was at the mercy of his emotions."[14] It was during the 1770s in poems like "The American Village," "The Beauties of Santa Cruz," and "The House of Night" that Freneau made his most noteworthy protests against the realities of life; in everything afterward he reluctantly compromised his ideals to the intellectual and artistic norms of his age. Picturing Freneau as the "young radical who never forgets his quarrel with a world which makes no room for him,"[15] Leary concludes that he "realized that his own failures, even the struggles of his country and the disruptions which threatened Europe, were all results of man's failure intelligently to adjust himself to the great and harmonious scheme of which he was a part."[16]

Although Leary's portrait of Freneau as an artistic as well as financial failure at the mercy of his feelings has not only worked its way into almost all the anthologies and surveys but undoubtedly has helped chill serious study of his poetry for the past thirty-five years, rivulets of interest have trickled on. In his 1949 monograph *Philip Freneau and the Cosmic Enigma*, Nelson F. Adkins attempted, as he says, to unravel "the various strands of philosophical and religious thought that thread their way through his works."[17] Adkins freely admits his project was designed to fill a gap in, not challenge the conclusions of, the Pattee-Clark-Leary interpretation; and although he draws many persuasive inferences from Freneau's poetry about the sources of his thought and suggests that Freneau's ideas were in some ways more substantial than had previously been thought, he concludes that Freneau's philosophy was cloudy and above all revealed "religious uncertainties" and "metaphysical gropings."[18] His thinking was a "tortuous path" on which he "swung from extreme to extreme in his search for truth."[19] Like the earlier commentators, Adkins suggests that, "had he lived in another age, his religious belief would have been more stable. But no age ever seethed with contending and conflicting modes of thought as the eighteenth century."[20] Similarly, Jacob Axelrad, in his 1967 biography *Philip Freneau: Champion of Democracy*, argues that Freneau was "easily inflammable . . . caught fire quickly, and was almost consumed while quenching the flames."[21] Basically an attempt to popularize Freneau by portraying him as a herald of liberal democracy and by freely inventing his day-to-day thoughts and feelings, Axelrad's book consistently relies on the earlier interpretation, as when it maintains that, though capable of "lofty lines and purity of thought," Freneau "lived in times which were often inimical to sustained effort on a high plane,"[22] or that in "a day when moral values were confused by political exigencies and artistic integrity suborned by political necessity" he was "peculiarly susceptible to the pressures of his time."[23] In short, Axelrad accepts the Pattee-Clark-Leary-Adkins portrait but excuses it by applauding Freneau's democratic faith.

Philip M. Marsh, who also published an admittedly "popular"[24] biography of Freneau in 1967, agrees with the traditional interpretation. Stressing Freneau's importance as a prose writer, Marsh says that he was a "biased, emotional, impractical, frustrated idealist—a dreamer, lover of beauty, of freedom, of peace."[25] In a descriptive essay on Freneau's writings, published in 1968, Marsh concludes that "somewhere in the controversies of the 1790s his at-times-delicate poetic genius had been blunted. He never wrote again as he had written occasionally before 1790."[26] Although Marsh repeatedly questions the negative conclusions of the earlier commentators and insists Freneau ought to be better known than he is, he not only fails to offer a counterinterpretation but in the main, as suggested above, accepts theirs.

In her recent study, Mary W. Bowden follows Marsh's lead in stressing Freneau's prose and in arguing that "Freneau's greatest claim to attention is the variety shown in his works."[27] Although disagreeing with the traditional view that Freneau was a romantic thwarted by the rationalism of his age, she agrees that his lyrics reveal "inconsistency in thought and a great variety in style, tone, and subject matter" and "all too often . . . lack unity and a single focus."[28] Although her insistence on Freneau's rationalism is a welcome corrective to earlier interpretations, the equation she implies between poetic symbol and irrationality, or what she at one point calls "mysticism,"[29] prevents her from examining Freneau's poems for meanings beyond the strictly literal. The result is a picture of Freneau that, however sympathetic at points, is on the whole even less flattering than the one drawn by Pattee, Clark, and Leary.

To summarize, then, the consensus portrait: Talented, but confused and unfocused, Freneau was a poet born in the wrong place and age. During the 1770s he strove to articulate his best poetic instincts in poems like "The American Village," "The House of Night," and "Santa Cruz," but lacking moral, intellectual, and emotional strength, he succumbed to the facts of the revolutionary era and sold his poetic birthright for political pottage. Impractical and impulsive, he failed to profit from this descent into worldly affairs, and despite his solid contributions to his country during the war and again in the 1790s, his countrymen dismissed him from their minds as soon as he finished each propagandistic campaign. The world was a puzzle to him throughout his life, much of which he spent groping for a financial and philosophical security he never found, and his political activism was in large part the result of personal and poetic inadequacies.

After long study of the evidence from which this portrait

has been drawn, I have reached substantially different conclusions. First, I have found a man whose search for the meaning of life was much more coherent, purposeful, and ultimately self-satisfying than has heretofore been suggested. Second, this search was conducted at an intensely private level almost wholly distinct from Freneau's public concerns. Third, the fruits of the search were expressed in roughly a hundred lyric poems, many of them unread today, that as a rule disguise Freneau's private thought behind various screens, suggesting that he not only resigned himself to total imperceptiveness on the part of his readers but may actually have tried to prevent discovery. Finally, his chief vehicle for expressing these thoughts was a system of private symbolism unique, so far as I can determine, in the poetry of the late eighteenth century.

The task of demonstrating that Freneau's most important poetic achievement was covert in nature is complicated by the fact that he himself not only exploited his reputation as a political propagandist in order to be as widely read as possible but often revised and manipulated his poems to the same end. No American poet has been a shrewder practitioner of the art of self-promotion. It is not hard to understand why, for example, he was in his lifetime and throughout the nineteenth century known almost exclusively as the Poet of the Revolution. In 1786 he titled his first book-length collection *Poems of Philip Freneau Written Chiefly during the Late War*, despite the fact that half the poems had nothing to do with the war. Again in 1809 he gave a new collection the equally misleading title *Poems Written and Published during the American Revolutionary War*. Fully two-thirds of this edition contradicted the title's claim. His final book was called *A Collection of Poems on American Affairs*, yet more than half its poems completely lacked the public, nationalistic flavor the title promised. Predictably, the first posthumous American edition, E. A. Duyckinck's 1865 *Poems Relating to the American Revolution*, included almost nothing but political pieces, and the first book-length biography, written by a Freneau descendant and published in 1902, was called *Philip Freneau: The Poet of the Revolution*. Samuel E. Forman reinforced the image by publishing a monograph titled "The Political Activities of Philip Freneau"[30] the same year. Only with the work of Pattee, Clark, and Leary was the image challenged, and they of course indirectly strengthened it by arguing he failed as a "pure" lyricist.

Yet the evidence of a symbolic intent is visible in scores of Freneau's poems. These hundred or so poems, written over a period of nearly fifty years, in effect constitute one poem that chronicles his intellectual and emotional evolution from youth to old age. Holding this poem together is a web of figures drawn from the classics, from the pastoral tradition, and from many other sources but dominated by a central pair of contrasting symbols — the land and the sea.

In 1961 Thomas J. Philbrick shrewdly observed that

Freneau's conception of the sea is neither clearcut nor simple. His view is not that of the eighteenth century, which, as we have noticed, saw the ocean as a destructive element that could be exploited for utilitarian purposes by the intelligence and energy of man; nor is it that of the romantics, who reveled in the power and vastness of the sea and viewed it as the emblem of sublimity and freedom. Freneau is fascinated by the sea, but this fascination stems less from its beauty than from its awful power and immensity. . . . In [his] conception of the voyage as ordeal, Freneau returned to the traditional center of efforts of the human imagination to read the meaning of maritime experience; the voyager becomes the type of all mankind in confrontation with the ultimate realities of life, realities that at once display man's capacity for nobility and lay bare his essential frailty.[31]

Philbrick is to date the only commentator to point out the symbolic quality of Freneau's treatment of the sea and to distinguish it from that of earlier British sea writers like Smollett, Falconer, and Dibdin. As he hints, the sea always connoted to Freneau the destructive, chaotic, inhuman aspects of nature manifested most tellingly to human beings in the fact of physical death. At the same time, it represented the restless, aggressive, ambitious, enterprising impulse—the impulse to know, to own, to domineer—and it emerges from his poems as an unmistakably male force.

On the other hand, Freneau always associated land with the benevolent, harmonious, passive aspects of nature, seeing its fecundity as the antithesis of ocean destructiveness and its gentleness as characteristically female. Annette Kolodny has recently uncovered evidence of this association in his political poetry, pointing out that

what Freneau consistently and insistently infused into [the personification of the new nation as feminine], however, was its inextricable connection to the larger femininity of soil and landscape, so that, whatever the ostensible object of the poem, the image of the nation as woman became one and the same with the image of the landscape.[32]

Although Kolodny shows that Freneau's political verse everywhere equates land and femaleness, in this study I shall also show that the most interesting and complex evidence of this is found in his nonpolitical lyrics, where he transforms the equation into private symbol and often directly contrasts it with the male sea. All the dozen or so intellectually definitive poems of his career, among them "The American Village," "The Beauties of Santa Cruz," "The Hurricane," "The Departure," "Hatteras," "Neversink," and "On Arriving in South Carolina," in some way juxtapose land and sea for the purpose of defining his understanding of human existence.

The female land-male sea polarity was a widespread phenomenon in American culture during the late eighteenth and early nineteenth centuries. Portraits of seagoing men were set against backgrounds of ships and the open sea; their wives, sisters, or daughters were invariably pictured in gardens, meadows, or woods. Benjamin West's 1809 painting *Telemachus and Calypso* balances the harsh sea from which Telemachus is stepping ashore with Calypso's soft and sensuously female island. Americans believed that the sea was too harsh and antisocial an environment for women and that only strong and resourceful men should challenge it.[33]

This attitude was in part the product of the idea diffused throughout western civilization since Homeric times that the sea was alien to humankind, an area of barbaric vagueness and chaos, which human beings entered only when necessary and then to cross as quickly as possible. More important, the attitude was also the product of the close contact with the sea that Americans had experienced since the earliest days of colonization. The New England puritans developed a complex mythos of ocean-crossing in which the voyage to America came to emblemize the spiritual trials that preceded the American saint's rebirth in the new Zion.[34] As the seaboard colonies grew during the seventeenth and eighteenth centuries, so did their dependence on the ships that provided most of their trade and transportation. By the outbreak of revolution in the 1770s, Americans had come not only to depend on the sea commercially but to view it as *the* American element on which future Americans would reap honor and profit from joint participation in various kinds of risk-taking ventures.[35] The ocean was thus as much a man's world to Freneau's culture as it had been to the ancient Greeks. What Freneau did in his poetry was to broaden its meaning until it symbolized for him the destructive forces of nature at war with the benign and female forces he associated with land.

His inspiration for doing so seems to have come from his experience as landsman and sailor rather than from literary models or precedents. In the work of no other eighteenth-century poet or critic before or contemporary with Freneau can a clear sign be found of Freneau's symbolic technique. The term "symbolism" was of course absent from the critical vocabulary of Freneau's day. Although terms like "trope" and "metaphor" were in common use, they denoted something very different from Freneau's method. Figurative language was used either ornamentally or to evoke precise mental pictures. As Chester Chapin, Patricia Spacks, and others have shown,[36] all the eighteenth-century British poets before Freneau subscribed to some form of the Lockeian theory that the mind drew its knowledge from the empirical world and that poetic images were, thus, either faithful reproductions of realities outside the poet's mind or recombinations by the poet of bits and pieces of external reality into original—i.e., unreal or fictional—creations. Although in the earlier part of the century both types of image-making were generally regarded as the product of poetic fancy or imagination, by midcentury poets and critics increasingly distinguished between the simple image, which was a faithful copy of nature, and the more complex image, which was a combination of parts of nature into poetic objects not found in nature. Poetry using the simple type of image was thought to appeal more to reason, and poetry using the complex type was thought to appeal more to fancy. By the time Freneau began publishing verse in the early 1770s, poets who held that fancy was superior to—more "poetic" and original than—reason and understanding dominated the British literary scene, and all of Freneau's poetry before 1780 clearly shows his commitment to their viewpoint.

Although these poets of fancy—among them the Wartons, Akenside, Gray, and Collins—strove for a more "creative" and "original" type of imagery in their art than earlier poets like Pope and Johnson had felt was true to nature or universal in experience, their work nevertheless contains no sign of the type of symbolic imagery, accumulating consistent meanings in single poems and in series of poems, that is found in Freneau's best work. One of the reasons that Freneau's originality in this respect has not been recognized is that in most other ways his poetry closely resembles theirs and that of the neoclassic tradition in general. In his nonpolitical poems, he tended not only to follow the generic approach which distinguished pastorals, odes, verse essays, dramatic essays, elegies, and other types from each other on the basis of accepted conventions of rhyme pattern, line and stanza structure, and narrative stance but also to use virtually all the conventional figurative techniques including periphrasis, prosopopoeia, and personification, which typify so-called eighteenth-century poetic diction.[37] Although this imitativeness was more pronounced during the 1770s, when he was under the sway of the school of fancy and was learning his craft, than afterward, it was nonetheless characteristic of his style throughout his career. In matters of form and diction, his poetry is unmistakably of the eighteenth century.

Yet it is at the same time remarkably original and modern in its fundamental aim of meeting the needs of its author rather than of its audience. Freneau's most significant foreshadowing of romantic and postromantic poetic technique lies not in his language or choice of subjects, as has often been argued, but rather in his internalization of poetic symbol, in the way his poetry reflects what Meyer Abrams has termed the shift from the pragmatic to the expressive theory of art in the late eighteenth and early nineteenth centuries.[38] In his best work, Freneau's central goal is not to copy nature or manipulate an audience but instead to express his own private state of mind and feeling at a given moment. He uses conventional eighteenth-century poetic techniques to convey complex, private meanings. The only other poet of his day to develop an at all comparable method was William Blake, whose birth and death dates virtually coincide with Freneau's. Yet Freneau's poetry reveals none of the overt symbolic mythopoesis of Blake's. Blake was a mystic, Freneau an empiricist; Blake tried to penetrate the secrets of the supernatural world, Freneau to make sense of the world of nature; Blake assumed the role of the prophet who was to reform mankind, Freneau the role of the private thinker who sought private conviction. Whereas Blake created a universe whose inhabitants and landscapes were obviously mythical and symbolic, Freneau never left the real world even in his most richly symbolic poems.

Despite his evidently wide reading before, during, and after college in ancient as well as modern literature, Freneau was raised in the aggressively pietistic atmosphere of American evangelical Calvinism, which Jonathan Edwards had helped create during the Great Awakening of the 1730s and 1740s. He was groomed for Princeton in the Reverend William Tennent's Manalapan grammar school, and his mother's parents were members of Tennent's church in Freehold. Tennent, who was acting president of Princeton at the time Freneau was a pupil in his grammar school, was the son of the founder of the radically evangelistic Log College in Neshaminy, Pennsylvania, and the brother of Gilbert Tennent, one of the most famous revivalist preachers of the Great Awakening and a close ally of Jonathan Edwards in the midcentury battles between New Light-New Side and Old Light-Old Side Calvinists.

The New Light-New Side movement was at the core a reaction against the inroads that secular Enlightenment thought had made in American Calvinism during the first half of the eighteenth century.[39] The empirical rationalism spawned by Newtonian science and Lockeian epistemology seriously eroded many American Calvinists' belief in humankind's ineluctable predestination to heaven or hell. Increasingly, in New England and the other colonies, Calvinists exposed to the new currents of thought began to question orthodox doctrine and to apply standards of human taste and reason to disputed matters of

faith. Good manners, breeding, and culture threatened to sup-
plant the soul-harrowing conversion experience as the chief
sign of grace. The Arminian notion that human beings were
free to choose salvation gained strength. Prudent, reasonable,
and moderate religious conduct was more admired than zeal.
Behind all these attitudinal shifts lay a profound change in the
concept of the deity itself: the inscrutable, despotic, yet intensely personal God of Calvin was giving way to the mathe-
matical, benign, yet remote Supreme Being of the deists and
freethinkers.

The New-Side and New-Light faction sought to return humankind to a passionate sense of communion in the mystical
body of Christ. Under the leadership of the Tennents and their
followers in the middle colonies, Princeton emerged in the
1740s as a New-Side stronghold. Although its most famous
evangelical president, Jonathan Edwards, died in 1758 before
he could formally take office, its other presidents held it on a
firmly evangelical course to the moment John Witherspoon
took the reins from Acting President Tennent, Freneau's men-
tor in Manalapan, and was installed just as Freneau was enter-
ing the college.

Witherspoon's tenure constituted a major turning point in
Princeton's intellectual history.[40] Although he had been recruited from Scotland because of his impeccable credentials
as an Evangelical in the Scottish church, Witherspoon's thinking was closer in many ways to that of the American Old Side
than to that of the New Siders who had controlled Princeton
since its founding in 1746. A major reason was that, although
the Scottish church had during the early decades of the eighteenth century divided into so-called Evangelical and Moderate
factions roughly paralleling the split between the New Side
and Old Side in America, its point of division was much nearer
the Enlightment end of the scale than was the point of division
in American Presbyterianism. A Moderate Calvinist in Scotland

was close to what most American Calvinists would regard as an out-and-out deist or freethinker, and an Evangelical was apt to be as "enlightened"as the average American Old-Side liberal. Francis Hutcheson, Professor of Moral Philosophy at Glasgow in the 1730s and 1740s and one of the leaders of the Scottish Moderates, was Jonathan Edwards's main target in *The Nature of True Virtue* (1754), in which Edwards in effect repudiated Hutcheson's entire theology. Yet John Witherspoon, brought to Princeton by the New Side to maintain the Edwardsian tradition only ten years after Edwards himself had been named president, not only accepted most of Hutcheson's ideas but taught them to his Princeton students, Freneau included, in his lectures on moral philosophy.[41]

In essence, Witherspoon taught Freneau the Scottish Common-Sense philosophy. Assuming that empirical reason and Christian revelation were entirely compatible, he maintained that in time all apparent contradictions between them would be resolved. His method was to outline for his students the various positions that had been taken on disputed theological and philosophical issues and then in effect to allow the students to reach their own conclusions, so sure was he that eventually empirical proof would be found for all points of orthodox doctrine. He was evidently not troubled by how close this came to a religion of reason because of his great faith, shared by virtually all Scottish thinkers of the eighteenth century, in the empirical method. It was to Witherspoon empirically demonstrable that humankind had an innate moral sense that infallibly knew right from wrong and was synonymous with conscience. Although his definition of conscience differed somewhat from Hutcheson's, Witherspoon agreed with Hutcheson that because God's moral law was inscribed directly on humankind's conscience it operated largely independently of formal creeds or philosophies. Experience with the real world—confrontation with solid empirical fact—was what led to genuine understanding of human fate. To Witherspoon, as to all the Scottish Common-Sense philosophers, abstract metaphysics and Cartesian rationalism were anathema. The kind of reason they respected was empirical, through which they believed human beings could learn to adapt to their environment and improve the spiritual as well as material conditions of life. Witherspoon continually extolled to his students the virtues of what he called plain common sense, by which he meant a combination of practical experience with the world and respect for time-tested institutions.

Witherspoon's empirico-pragmatic philosophical bias appears to have influenced Freneau deeply. It seems in the first place to have immediately swept away whatever New-Side enthusiasm his parents and William Tennent had managed to instill in him before he entered Princeton. That Freneau was not born to the evangelical ministry seems so obvious from everything he afterward did as to make it almost impossible not to think that hearing Witherspoon's worldly, reasonable lectures came as the most pleasant shock of his young intellectual life. In addition, Witherspoon appears to have inadvertently set in motion the chain of repudiations that led Freneau to burst out sometime during 1773-74, "And so Farewell to the study of Divinity —which is, in fact, the Study of Nothing! —and the profession of a priest is little better than that of a slothful Blockhead!"[42] About the time of the outburst, Freneau also evidently abandoned Christianity itself for good.

But Witherspoon's most important influence on Freneau is found in the epistemological assumptions of the poetry Freneau published after 1780. Although his poems of the 1770s are saturated with a nebulous idealism and the pro-fancy bias of the midcentury preromantic poets already mentioned, all his post-1780 poetry reflects a pragmatic realism virtually indistinguishable from that of Witherspoon and his Scottish Common-Sense predecessors—minus, of course, their Christian focus. Freneau's focus is, instead, unvarnished temporal reality and the harshly inexorable processes of nature, especially death. It is as though Freneau returns, after a brief infatuation with poetic fancy, to Witherspoon's plain common sense and to the empiricism on which it rested. Although Freneau's Calvinistic background does not seem to have directly influenced his symbolic method, except insofar as it acquainted him with the typological method of reading scripture,[43] it nevertheless provided him, mainly through Witherspoon, with a highly pragmatic intellectual framework within which to develop a poetic method more personal and symbolically complex than that of his fellow poets writing in English.

Freneau's methodological breakthrough was not unlike that of another American artist of the revolutionary period, John Singleton Copley, who in 1778 painted his celebrated *Watson and the Shark*. In a brilliant analysis, Roger B. Stein[44] shows that Copley, in applying the techniques of the grand European style of religious and historical painting to a single catastrophic event in the life of an ordinary individual—a shark attack on the English merchant Brook Watson in Havana harbor—not only helped shift the subject matter of painting from the divine or heroic to the secular and mundane but also epitomized the experimentalism and innovativeness that permeated American intellectual and artistic life during the revolutionary era. The painting places a common American boatman in the central position traditionally reserved for Christ or classical heroes and thus, as Stein says, reflects "the revolution [in] history painting which was taking place in the 1770s, spearheaded by Americans like West and Copley, whose aesthetic premises were . . . open, flexible, and experimental."[45]

So too Freneau's. In charging his lyric poetry with private symbolic meaning, Freneau was both challenging the generic assumptions that dominated the neoclassical tradition he inherited and foreshadowing the central literary technique of the American Renaissance of the 1840s and 1850s. It has often been said of Freneau as a kind of reproach that he influenced no one, had no following, created no school: later writers like Emerson, Thoreau, Whitman, Hawthorne, and Melville hardly knew who he was. Although probably accurate in one sense, such criticism wholly misses the mark as far as Freneau's importance in the development of American symbolic literature is concerned. In his own day and manner, he was at least as original and uniquely "American" as they.

The philosophical conclusions that he expressed through his symbols evolved slowly, often painfully, but with remarkable consistency over a period of many years. Emotionally and intellectually committed during the 1770s to a fancy-oriented eighteenth-century romanticism, he expressed a belief in the poems he published before 1780 that fancy was superior to reason and provided a groundwork not merely for a poetry that idealized nature but for a lifestyle that eschewed the humdrum of ordinary life. But after 1780 the fancy-reason pendulum swung the other way, until by the mideighties Freneau had concluded that fancy and the pastoral, female landscapes he associated with it were delusive and that only the ocean and the rationalistic stoicism it taught were real. The philosophical implications of this swing in point of view were extremely unsettling. Land bred every kind of illusion, including religious fables that promised life after death. The ocean, on the other hand, ruthlessly destroyed such illusions, suggesting that nature was at the core blank, indifferent, and meaningless.

Freneau's leaving of the sea in the late eighties for married life on land was accompanied by a series of poems that not only reassessed the relative values of land and sea but, more importantly, distinguished them both from ultimate reality, which by 1791 Freneau had located in a realm of immutable reason beyond physical nature. Land and sea, warmth and cold, calm and storm, and life and death were only superficial, not absolute, dichotomies in a fundamentally reasonable and stable universe. Neither pole of any of the dichotomies was more or less real or valuable than its opposite: all were equally necessary to the cosmic design. For the rest of his life, Freneau held unwaveringly to this philosophical compromise.

The most intensely symbolic period of his poetic career was thus the decade between 1780 and 1790. These were his ten years of greatest intellectual ferment, during which he twice revised his philosophy of life. Before 1780, he published a mere handful of poems, and of this handful only a half-dozen were significantly nonpolitical. After 1790 he turned from a private to a more public poetic mode, apparently largely as a result of having resolved the private philosophical doubts that had plagued him during the eighties. Accordingly, this study focuses on the poems of that decade, though it does so, of course, for the purpose of establishing the lasting importance of his entire literary career.

Since no satisfactory edition of his poems exists and only sporadic efforts have been made to account for his revisions, considerable attention will be paid here to the chronology of his publishing and revising. Two points concerning this chronology should be made at once. First, Freneau's poems almost invariably reflect the thought and technique of the period in which they were first published, no matter what compositional dates Freneau either openly or implicitly gave them. Throughout his career and especially in the 1795 collection, he tried to create the impression he had been a successful and widely-published poet since college by backdating to the 1770s poems published after 1780. Although some of these poems were doubtless first drafted in the seventies, most—even the ones drafted early—were substantially the product of the period when they were first issued.

Second, there are unmistakable signs in his revising of an effort to remove personal or topical elements from newspaper versions for the collected editions and of a corresponding effort to broaden and deepen their meaning. However, in the 1795 and 1809 editions Freneau tried to bring many of the pessimistic poems already collected in the 1786 and 1788 editions into line with the optimism of his post-1790 philosophy, notably softening them in the process. Thus as a rule, the most interesting and reliable version of a poem is the one found in the earliest collected edition. Accordingly, though this study follows the chronology of earliest publication as the central thread of Freneau's intellectual development, it uses later versions as guidelines to the meaning of the originals whenever appropriate.

The evidence that Freneau expressed a small fraction of his literary energies in his public poems and that his deepest thought and feeling flowed into his private lyrics lies in the lyrics themselves. Corroborative proof — a direct statement, for instance, by Freneau in a letter, journal, or manuscript of a symbolic intention — has not been and probably never will be found. The fire that destroyed his Mt. Pleasant home in 1818 and with it almost all his personal papers may also have destroyed such evidence, if it existed. Yet his refusal to acknowledge such an intention openly, a refusal that has diverted attention from some of his most rewarding poems to many that are merely topical or stylistically clever, is perhaps not so eccentric as it seems. A number of other American writers raised, like Freneau, in a Calvinistic milieu, have been equally secretive — witness Edward Taylor's injunction against publication, Melville's lonely and defiant pursuit of private goals after *Moby Dick*, Emily Dickinson's solitary labors in Amherst. Freneau was, after all, an unconventional thinker in an age and society acutely suspicious of unconventionality. Constantly exploring the meaning of land and sea in his lyric verse and relating them to other less pervasive metaphors, he moved in the course of his career from romantic idealism through a period of corrosive skepticism to a faith in the rationality of nature. What follows is the record of this spiritual journey.

II

"My Fav'rite Isle
to Ruin Gone," 1772-1779

Of the half-dozen important lyric poems he published before 1780, Freneau reprinted only two, "Columbus to Ferdinand" and "The Dying Elm," in roughly original form in later editions. He never reprinted "The American Village"; he reduced "The Farmer's Winter Evening" from a serious pastoral to a burlesque; he ultimately discarded all but a half-dozen stanzas of "The House of Night"; and he completely reversed the argument of "The Beauties of Santa Cruz." "The Dying Elm" was expanded from three quatrains to four, considerably changing its meaning.

The poems of no subsequent period suffered such harsh treatment. Much of his later dissatisfaction with these early poems seems to have stemmed from the fact they expressed an idealized view of nature that he renounced after 1780. Furthermore, they argued that poetry was, or ought to be, the product of the kind of fancy celebrated by Joseph Warton, William Collins, Thomas Gray, and almost all other midcentury British poets—a fancy that romanticized nature and tended to purge it of unpleasantness. Finally, all of them but "The Dying Elm" were unguarded efforts in which he more or less wore his heart on his sleeve. Only "The Dying Elm" employed the oblique and indirect style of his mature work.

His first independent book of verse was published in 1772, when he was twenty. The longest of its four poems, the 438-line title piece "The American Village," contains a passage as openly symbolic as any he ever committed to print. Freneau leads up to the passage by contrasting the Auburn of Goldsmith's just-published "The Deserted Village" with the prosperous village typical of rural America. Then at line 86 the poem suddenly breaks and sets forth a remarkable seventy-six-line description of an island somewhere "Between New-Albion and the Mexic' Bay."[1] Although the speaker here sets the island in a more or less specific geographical locale, the information he gives us about it in the rest of the passage requires us to see virtually the whole description as imaginary. Beginning with the ambiguous comment that "A lovely island once adorn'd the sea" (1. 87), he proceeds to picture the island in a lush primeval state, covered with plant and animal life. This leads him to an equally fanciful description of a community of shepherds living in peace and contentment on the island. It is not until the last eight of the seventy-six lines that he explains that the island is now, in the poem's present, nothing but a bar of sand:

> *But envious time conspiring with the sea,*
> *Wash'd all it's landscapes, and it's groves away.*
> *It's trees declining, stretch'd upon the sand,*
> *No more their shadows throw across the land.*
> *It's vines no more their clust'ring beauty show,*
> *Nor sturdy oaks embrace the mountain's brow.*
> *Bare sands alone now overwhelm the coast,*
> *Lost in* [sic] *it's grandeur, and it's beauty lost.*
>
> (11. 155-62)

The rest of the seventy-six lines similarly suggest that Freneau intended the island to symbolize the benign, harmonious, and gentle aspects of nature. As already mentioned, the speaker begins by visualizing the island in a paradisiacal wilderness state. Covered with oaks, hazels, alders, aspens, and plum trees and inhabited only by birds and herbivorous animals, it signifies beneficent natural forces. At its center is a fountain of fresh water, which connotes purity and rejuvenation but which is, ominously, "quickly in the salter ocean drown'd" (1. 114). It is "the happy isle" (1. 92), not merely "peaceful" (1. 101) but "sacred" (1. 117). In this initial image Freneau paints a perfect state of nature. Although the ocean surges against it in "conclusive throws" (1.95), foreshadowing its ultimate destruction, and swallows up its fresh water, the island itself is idyllic because, as the speaker carefully points out, "no men were here" (1. 108). Freneau introduces human beings into this symbolic setting through his second symbolic image — that of a village completely isolated from the rest of the world and inhabited by a primitive race "with happy ignorance divinely blest" (1. 141). By arguing that the island was a paradise only when "no men were here" and then contradictorily painting an idyllic pastoral community on it, he seems not only to deny that human beings ever did or could exist in such a perfect state of nature but again to point to the island's inevitable decay.

Freneau concludes his account of the island and introduces the next section of "The American Village" with lines that cast a flood of light on his treatment of the pastoral-primitivistic theme for the rest of his literary career:

> *Thus, tho' my fav'rite isle to ruin gone,*
> *Inspires my sorrow, and demands my moan;*
> *Yet this wide land it's place can well supply*
> *With landscapes, hills and grassy mountains high.*
>
> (11. 163-66)

The island is Freneau's "fav'rite" locale in a metaphoric sense. For him its charm lies in its representation, first, of a natural harmony unmarred by temporal decay and, second and much more tentatively, the possibility of a participation in this harmony by an abnormally innocent type of person. The requirements of the second possibility are so stringent — spontaneous generation of a race of human beings on the island, their total isolation from the rest of humankind, a vegetable-like lack of curiosity on their part about natural phenomena, no development or change from within the island society over the ages, no contemplation of the mysteries of life and death — as to make it seem not merely whimsical but repellent, the speaker's characterization of these islanders as "souls sublime" (1. 153) notwithstanding. With startling openness, Freneau maps out in these four lines what became a lifelong procedure: since the realities of mortal life (the physical decay symbolized by the inevitable erosion of the island by the sea) rule out the possibility of a truly harmonious relation between human beings and nature, Freneau will celebrate a pastoral and relatively benign America ("This wide land") as a socially and politically useful second choice. Freneau's promulgation of an agrarian, quasi-primitivist political myth for America during the course of the next forty years stemmed from a decision reflected in these lines and was cool, premeditated, and in a sense manipulative from beginning to end. Kenneth Silverman has observed that Freneau "withheld devotion from the causes he espoused."[2] "The American Village" reveals that he had rejected primitivism as a serious poetic or philosophical creed by 1772 but had understood its usefulness as political and social propaganda. The reams of primitivist verse and prose, including most of the Pilgrim and Tomo Cheeki essays, which he ground out in subsequent decades, were consciously superficial. His real artistic energies were at work elsewhere.

This is not to suggest that he did not believe in the political myth that he as much as any other American of his generation helped promulgate. It is only to claim that the myth never met his demands for a world view that could comprehend the elemental conflicts and contradictions he sensed in the empirical universe around him. Privately, apparently with no recognition by his contemporaries of what he was trying to do, he wrote poem after poem in ensuing years in which he grappled with these deeper problems. Although written in the pastoral mode, "The American Village" actually denies the central assumption of the classical pastoral tradition—that a harmonious and deeply satisfying way of life is recoverable in the country, close to nature—and argues that nature is no less transient and mutable than humankind. Only in a wilderness unapproachable except in fancy—like the island as the speaker of "The American Village" imagines it before it was washed away—is nature at harmony with itself.

Aside from its island passage, "The American Village" is generally propagandistic in the manner of Freneau's later primitivist efforts.[3] Although perhaps not one of his masterpieces, it is at least the equal of many he included in his later collections and, at least in the island passage, provides an indispensable clue to the meaning of many of his most important later poems. Why did he never acknowledge it through republication? The argument that he was so wounded by hostile criticism of the poem that he suppressed it—an argument resting solely on his remark in a letter to Madison November 22, 1772, that the volume was out and was "damned by all good and judicious judges"[4]—provides only a partial answer. Equally significant is that by the time he put his first collection together in the mideighties he seems to have found the blatantly symbolic approach of the island passage too crude. He had by that time developed a far more oblique method, as we shall see, and perhaps he wanted to keep the relatively obvious "American Village" out of sight. It may have struck him as too easy an entrée into what he had come to regard, perhaps perversely and certainly pridefully, as no one's property but his own. Like Taylor,

Melville, and Dickinson, he had apparently decided he was his own best audience. Also, he had abandoned the romanticism that permeates "The American Village." Although the poem implies that the human longing for natural paradise is unfulfillable, it also implies that the vision of a harmonious, uncorrupted state of nature has genuine poetic validity. The final fifty lines fantasize about withdrawing from human society and taking up a hermitlike life of contemplation in the woods. The hermit's only diversion would be the "darling sin" (1. 414) of reading the poetry of secular writers like Shakespeare, Dryden, Pope, and Addison. Although humorous, the fantasy implies that total isolation in the wilderness might possibly reveal a glimpse of nature's benevolent heart.

A similar note is struck in "The Farmer's Winter Evening, A Poem: To the Nymph I never saw," which immediately follows "The American Village" in the 1772 volume. After sketching a picture of a forest cottage in which a group of "jovial swains, with heart sincere"[5] swap stories on a winter night, the speaker launches into a passionate address to a "pretty rural shepherdess" (1. 48) who turns out to be the imaginary nymph of the poem's subtitle. If he could live with this "FLORA" (1. 60) in his "fancy'd wood" (1. 46), he says,

> *Then sacred groves, and shades divine,*
> *And all ARCADIA should be mine.*
>
> (11. 51-52)

In other words, marriage to this mysterious Flora, whose name signifies the Roman goddess of flowers or, more broadly, plant life in general, would transform the "fancy'd wood" into a "sacred" and "divine" region resembling the happy island of "The American Village." Flora seems to be another metaphor for beneficent nature, marriage to her another metaphor for communion with it. Here Freneau not only associates these happy forces with land, as on the island of "The American

Village," but for the first time specifically links them with femaleness.

The poem further invites a metaphorical reading of the marriage when in its closing lines the speaker makes his strange call for opiates to dissolve the real world and unite him with his Flora. After finding an imaginary first taste of opium too weak, he demands

> *A larger draught, a larger bowl*
> *To gratify my drowsy soul;*
> *'A larger draught is yet in store,*
> *Perhaps with this you wake no more.'*
> *Then I my lovely maid shall see thee*
> *Drinking the deep streams of LETHE,*
> *Where now dame ARETHUSA scatters*
> *Her soft stream with ALPHEUS' waters,*
> *To forget her earthly cares,*
> *Lost in LETHE, lost in years!*
> *And I too will quaff the water,*
> *Lest it should be said, O daughter*
> *Of my giddy, wand'ring brain,*
> *I sigh'd for one I've never seen.*
>
> (ll. 61-74)

The two quoted lines are evidently spoken by Flora herself. The entire poem leads up to her ambiguously oracular answer to his increasingly frantic demands, and the lines he speaks immediately after hers are his reply. What she says, in effect, is that the only chance he has to win her is to die and thus to escape mortality altogether. Her unequivocal assertion that a "larger draught is yet in store" almost surely refers to death, the ultimate narcotic. Her chilling hint that he may never awaken—in other words, that there is no life beyond physical death—both expresses for Freneau a lifelong doubt concerning the soul's immortality and questions whether the longed-for communion with nature takes place after death.

The speaker's response to Flora's comment, occupying the last ten lines of the poem, bulges with meaning. He grants the likelihood that there will be no life or enlightenment after death but argues that Flora's, i.e., nature's, impercipience — her drinking the waters of Lethe — will mingle with his own like the waters of the sacred springs Alpheus and Arethusa. Probably thinking of Ovid's version, the only full one in classical literature,[6] Freneau insinuates that the relationship between the speaker of the poem and his imaginary Flora is like the relationship between these two mythical rivers. The spring Alpheus, source of the principal river in classical Arcadia, fell in love with and approached Arethusa, a mortal dedicated to Artemis, goddess of the wilderness. Terrified, Arethusa ran away, but Alpheus chased her until, exhausted, she called to Artemis for help. Artemis changed her into a river and made a tunnel for her to escape under the ocean from Greece to Sicily, where she became a fountain sacred to Artemis. Alpheus followed, however, and mingled with her. To this fable Freneau adds the widely held classical notion that all rivers, including Lethe, the river of forgetfulness, ultimately run together in the subterranean kingdom of Hades, or death. He suggests his speaker's pursuit of Flora, like Alpheus' pursuit of the Artemis wilderness principle, may be consummated by a return to the oblivion and insensibility of the nonhuman natural order through death. Yet he does not present this as an unpleasant or disagreeable possibility: it will be at worst a reunification with classical pagan serenities.[7] Finding Flora, his elusive ideal of nature, metaphorically drinking the waters of oblivion, he too will gladly drink, "Lest it should be said . . . I sigh'd for one I've never seen." These striking lines seem to express some defiance toward the Christian view of nature that denies the possibility or the value of the kind of communion with nature the speaker craves. Rather than simply accept such a view, the speaker seems to be saying, I am willing to die and find out the truth first hand.

In these two early poems, published before he reached legal manhood, Freneau sketched the outlines of a pastoral, fancy-oriented vision that dominated the lyric verse he published during the seventies. The central argument of the poems is that although human beings cannot hope to communicate fully with the benign forces of nature during their natural lives and may well join them merely in "dread nihility," as he terms it in "The American Village" (1. 383), after death, these forces are beautiful and enthralling enough to justify a deep poetic commitment. The nearest approach a mortal can make to them is in the undisturbed wilderness on land where plant life and the lower forms of animal life exist in a harmony somewhat analogous to the transcendent and invisible harmonies that create and sustain empirical nature. Although "The American Village" emblemizes the ocean as the force in physical nature that precludes humankind's realizing the vision on earth, the poem does not suggest the possibility that the ocean may invalidate the vision in any ultimate sense. The island suffers ruin only in the realm of reason and empirical fact, not in the realm of poetic fancy.

Nearly seven years passed after *The American Village* volume before Freneau published another poem that was not propagandistic in aim. Then, in the course of 1779, four poems having little to do with the revolution appeared in Hugh Henry Brackenridge's *United States Magazine*. Of these, "The House of Night; or Six Hours Lodging with Death: A Vision" is probably the earliest written and certainly the most peculiar. As is often the case with Freneau's poems, "The House of Night," even in this earliest version, shows signs of having been put together at different times. The setting, twice identified as the Chesapeake Bay region,[8] strongly hints that the poem was first written during Freneau's 1773-74 stint with Brackenridge at Somerset Academy in Maryland, as do the closing lines, which identify the speaker as being twenty-three years old.

Yet stanzas 39-45 make anachronistic reference to the war and England's use of Hessian troops, indicating that at least parts of this section of the poem could not have been written before 1776. Probably Freneau wrote a draft of the poem while or shortly after he was in Maryland, then revised it in 1778 or 1779 for publication in the *United States Magazine*.

The poem's main interest lies in its commitment to the theory of fancy current among the leading British poets of the day. Freneau openly calls the poem a "Vision," which he makes no attempt to justify or explain, insisting throughout that the narrative—a lurid account of Death's death on the shores of the Chesapeake Bay—was nothing but a dream. His only argument is that "Poetic dreams are of a finer cast/Than those which o'er the sober brain diffus'd,/Are but a repetition of some action past" (11. 6-8)—that is, in protest against the descriptive imagery of poets earlier in the century, that fancy, or imagination, is capable of synthesizing empirical data into sublimely impressive images not found in nature. All his repeated references to fancy in the opening and closing stanzas[9] conform to current romantic usage: fancy produces original, creative, and stimulating "dreams" or "visions" like those of "The House of Night," and reason slavishly copies reality.

A more significant poem in the development of Freneau's own symbolic method was "The Beauties of Santa Cruz," first published without title in the February 1779 issue of the *United States Magazine* along with a prefatory prose "Account of the Island of Santa Cruz."[10] According to this prose introduction, the poem was "composed near two years ago on the spot"[11] — in other words, around the beginning of 1777, in the middle of Freneau's West-Indies sojourn. As in "The American Village," this first version of "Santa Cruz" idealizes the pastoral felicities of an island. However, this is not a fancied but a real island, to which the speaker invites every "northern . . . shepherd" (1. 1) who may read the poem. Completely missing is the exclusiveness and rigor of the pastoral ideal defined in "The American Village" and "The Farmer's Winter Evening." Freneau throws Santa Cruz open to the tourists. Nowhere is the tropical landscape presented as anything more than a sort of recreational diversion for anyone who wants to visit it.

The island is already populated with rich planters engaged in "commerce" (1. 127) based on slavery: the "Ethiopian swain" (1. 149) on the island longs for "a land of freedom and repose,/Where cruel slavery never sought to reign" (11. 153-4). Plainly this is no paradise, no retreat where one can hope to commune with a beneficent wilderness. The speaker's continual hints of a paradiselike virtue in Santa Cruz—its "perpetual green" (1. 10), its "gay enchanting shore" (1. 16), its resemblance to "Eden's ground" (1. 80), its "inchanting juice" (of the sugar cane) as tempting as the "Lotos" (11. 137 and 143), and its likeness to a "land of love" (1. 196)—are purely ornamental. The truth of the matter is that to the speaker these virtues are soporific, as he points out in the sixth stanza when he says that "reason's voice must whisper to *the soul* / That nobler climes for man the Gods design" (11. 21-22). Besides, hurricanes periodically ravage the island, revealing "Nature convuls'd in every form of woe" (1. 160) and partly fulfilling the ever-present potential for destructiveness of the "threatening waters" of the ocean that "roar on every side" (1. 27).

The speaker feels guilty about staying on the island. "Fain would I view," he says, "my native climes again,"

> But murder marks the cruel Briton there—
> Contented here I rest, in spite of pain,
> And quaff the enlivening juice in spite of care.
>
> (11. 177-80)

A stanza later he asks rhetorically why one should let gloomy thoughts "cloud the sunshine of the mind" (1. 184) if one is in a happy place like Santa Cruz, suggesting he is having precisely

those thoughts. Almost defiantly he insists in the next stanza
that "Night and its kindred glooms are nought to me" (1. 188).
This is because, even though day and night do alternate,

> *Tomorrow's sun new paints the faded scene;*
> *Though deep in ocean sink his western beams,*
> *His spangled chariot shall arise more clear,*
> *More radiant from the drowsy land of dreams.*
>
> (11. 189-92)

The rationale offered here for maintaining the eroded pastoral
stance struck in the poem as a whole does not seem to convince
the speaker himself. Although the mind periodically darkens
like the night, it inevitably brightens like the day and paints
things in their true, cheerful colors. Gloomy thoughts are insubstantial products of a "drowsy land of dreams." The speaker's
diffidence is obvious in the poem's last four stanzas, where he
invites northerners one last time to come to Santa Cruz, assumes few or none will, and ends by asserting that even if they
do not he, "pleas'd," will remain and "sing with rapture" the
island's "inspiring shades" (11. 207-8).

The 1779 version of "Santa Cruz" shows that Freneau was
by 1777 clinging halfheartedly to the shreds of a pastoral ideal
he had as early as 1772 decided was unworkable as a serious
personal philosphy of life, however attractive in poetic fancy.
The island of Santa Cruz represents to him a sort of vacation
from serious concerns and is so presented to the shepherds it
is supposed to entice. It is a narcotic, like the Lotos-land it is
compared to, temporarily to ease the pain of patriots—and of
poets. The fact that he makes it accessible to everyone shows
how cheap it is in comparison to the high price of the imaginary
island in "The American Village." The baroque effect of the
poem's natural descriptions, which Leary has noted,[12] is a
symptom of this fundamental tawdriness. Although Freneau's
revisions for the 1786 edition conformed the poem to his ma-

ture thought, as will be seen, they could not completely cure it of its original ills. The fact that it argues for a moral position Freneau himself had abandoned at least a year before it was published suggests the emotional and intellectual confusion of his entire Caribbean adventure.

However, the third of the four key poems Freneau published in the *United States Magazine*, "Columbus to Ferdinand," reveals an important new theme, one basic to much of the poetry he published afterward. Although "The Rising Glory of America," a turgid paean to America's future written jointly by Freneau and Brackenridge for their Princeton commencement and published in pamphlet form in 1772, mentions ocean trade as one of America's probable strengths, it pays almost no attention to the ocean.[13] And though both "The American Village" and "Santa Cruz" image the ocean as a force antithetical to the islands it surrounds, neither seriously probes its meaning. With the figure of Columbus in "Columbus to Ferdinand," Freneau begins work on the complicated nexus of ideas that he wove around fresh as well as salt water during the course of the next dozen years.

The poem pictures Columbus at the beginning of his career pleading with Ferdinand to sponsor a voyage of exploration into the unknown seas west of Europe. His appeal is almost exclusively to Ferdinand's reason and sense of intellectual adventure. He argues first that it is unreasonable to assume there is nothing but water between the west coast of Europe and the east coast of Asia, an assumption that covers the earth disproportionately with ocean. God is a more intelligent and orderly architect than that.[14] Next Columbus invokes the oracle of reason, Plato, who predicted that in time lands undreamed of would be found beyond "The Hibride isles or Caledonia's shore" (1. 36). Finally he cites the recent invention of the compass as solving the navigational problems of such a voyage and points to centuries of practical sailing experience on the Mediterranean as providing the needful shipbuilding know-how (11. 41-52). Twice Columbus says that, on the voyage he contemplates, "Reason shall steer and skill disarm the gale" (11. 40 and 56).

The word fancy appears nowhere in the poem. Columbus's speculations are identified solely with reason. Evidently, by the late seventies Freneau had already begun associating the figure of the seagoing explorer with a realism and rationalism alien to the poet who yearned for islands of the heart's desire. Although no such distinction is explicitly stated in the poem, it is implicit in Columbus's whole character. Unlike the speakers of "The American Village," "The Farmer's Winter Evening," and "Santa Cruz," he is a man of action bent on verifying his fancies with hard fact. Moreover, he represents virtues diametrically opposed to those of the imaginary shepherds on the "American Village" island. He is dynamic; they are passive. He seeks danger; they seek safety. He thrives on new knowledge; they thrive on blissful ignorance. He is ocean-oriented; they cling to land. By the mideighties voyagers like him had effectively supplanted shepherds like them as Freneau's moral ideal.

The most interesting and suggestive lyric Freneau published before 1780 is, characteristically, the shortest and least pretentious in appearance. Immediately before "Columbus to Ferdinand," in the June 1779 issue of the *United States Magazine*, appears "The Dying Elm, An Irregular Ode." I quote it in full.

> *Sweet, lovely elm, who here dost grow,*
>   *Companion of my musing care;*
> *Lo, thy dejected branches die,*
>   *Amid the burning air;*
> *Smit by the sun or sickly moon,*
> *Like fainting flow'rs that die at noon.*

Thy withering leaves that drooping hang,
  Presage thy end approaching nigh,
And lo, thy amber tears distil,
  Attended with thy last remaining sigh.
O gentle tree no more decline,
But be thy shade and love-sick whispers mine.

Short is thy life if thou so soon must fade,
  Like angry Jonah's gourd at Nineveh,
That in a night its bloomy branches spread,
  And flourish'd for a day.
Come, then revive, sweet shady elm, lest I,
Thro' vehemence of heat, like Jonah, wish to die.[15]

On its face, the poem seems to be a rather sentimental lament for a favorite elm that is dying of a disease exacerbated by a heat wave. The detail of the "amber tears," presumably a saplike antitoxin oozing out of the tree's bark, reinforces this literalness. Yet the fact that the speaker addresses a natural object recalls Freneau's argument in "The American Village" and "The Farmer's Winter Evening" that genuine empathy with nature, though desirable, is impossible in the real world. Here and in a number of later poems like "The Wild Honey-Suckle" and "The Man of Ninety" the speaker talks to and projects emotions onto a plant that not only does not respond but that Freneau implies cannot respond. Although here he does not reprimand the speaker for sentimentalizing dumb nature, in a number of later poems Freneau treats this human tendency as one more proof of the human capacity for self-deception. In 1779 he was apparently still enough of a romanticist to allow a speaker to talk without self-consciousness to a tree.

One of the keys to the poem's meaning lies in its final stanza. The elaborate comparison there between the speaker's relation to the elm and Jonah's relation to the gourd tree suggests that Freneau is likening his own situation in the late 1770s to Jonah's at Nineveh. Jonah, it will be recalled, enraged by God's dragging him to Nineveh against his will and then deciding not to destroy Nineveh and thereby making him appear to be a false prophet, goes out to the desert to sulk. To teach him a lesson, God grows a shade tree for him, which He then kills, exposing Jonah to the sun. By then comparing Jonah's pity for the shade tree with His own pity for Nineveh, God brings home to Jonah the need for compassion even for one's enemies. Similarly, Freneau had since 1775 been publishing verse diatribes against the British. Like Jonah, he had assumed the role of a denunciatory prophet predicting the ruin of a British-ruled America, though even in his most virulent anti-British poems of the seventies, as one critic recently remarked, he "refused to serve as some sloganeering firebrand; he made his abhorrence of British policy serve his wish to write the poetry of fancy."[16] The final stanza of "The Dying Elm" wittily reveals that Freneau was no more enthusiastic than Jonah for the job of prophesying doom.

The relevance of the Jonah-compassion motif to Freneau is further clarified by the other key to the poem's meaning, the tree Freneau chose as his subject. Freneau's awareness of the sacredness of certain trees in classical tradition is probably reflected in his enumeration of various types of trees on the symbolic island of "The American Village." Among the trees sacred to the Greeks and Romans, the elm, along with the cypress and white poplar, was generally associated with death and the underworld and was often used to decorate burial grounds.[17] That Freneau had this association in mind in 1779 is shown by his reference to "the church-yard elm" (1. 35) in "The House of Night." Further, in addition to this general association, he was familiar with Virgil's description of the elm that stands inside the entrance to the underworld in Book VI of *The Aeneid*:

In the open a huge dark elm tree spreads wide its immemorial
Branches like arms, whereon, according to old wives' tales,
Roost the unsolid Dreams, clinging everywhere under
    its foliage.[18]

This association of the elm tree with dreams, well enough established in classical mythology to allow Virgil to incorporate
it in *The Aeneid* as a "fact," underlies Freneau's use of the
elm in the poem. Like Virgil's, his elm is also a tree of dreams,
although for Freneau, as his calling the tree the "companion"
of his "musing" care in line 2 suggests, the "sweet, lovely elm"
evidently represents his own poetic dreams and thus his nonpolitical and nonpropagandistic poetic impulses — for instance,
the "dreams,/Of fields and woods, and running streams" (11.
57-58) he celebrates in "The Farmer's Winter Evening" and the
"poetic dreams" he ranks above all other kinds in the second
stanza of "The House of Night." Instead of picturing these
poetic impulses as birds nesting in his elm, as Virgil does with
the dreams in his, Freneau associates them generally with the
tree itself and specifically with its leaves. Attacking the tree are
"the burning air," "the sun," and the "sickly moon." The
hot weather is evidently a metaphor for the partisan, often
satiric, political poetry he had been publishing since 1775 and,
beyond that, for the whole feverish climate of war and revolution that he evidently felt was blighting his better poetic instincts.

The witty allusion to Jonah in the final stanza clinches the
poem's argument. Like Jonah, Freneau stands to be burned
up "thro' vehemence of heat" — in one sense his own partisan
literary violence — if his lyric sensibility, the elm tree (Jonah's
gourd tree), dies in the heat and glare. He has been metaphorically shaded from total partisanship until now by this gentler
and more attractive side of his poetry, but he is afraid his tree,
like Jonah's, is withering. In his wry yet alarmed comment,

"Short is thy life if thou so soon must fade," he reviews his career in lyric verse and implies it has not been everything he had hoped for. He begs it to "revive" out of a fear that if it does not he will lose all perspective and become the self-righteous, humorless, and cruel crier for blood and vengeance whom he poses as in his political poems and whom the figure of Jonah under the gourd tree at Nineveh so fittingly recalls.

Jonah's learning the value of pity can thus be seen as central to the point Freneau is trying to make. In asking for the tree's "shade and love-sick whispers" to be his, Freneau is on one level making a relatively straightforward request for lyric inspiration. More important, he is also suggesting that love is, or ought to be, a key concern of the poetry he wants to write. The current climate, metaphorically considered, he sees as one of rancor, discord, and hatred. The "burning air" of the dry spell connotes the heartless atmosphere of the war and of his own propagandistic crudeness. He is suffering through a general drought of human compassion that leaves the affectionate side of his personality, like the tree, "fainting," "withering," and "drooping."

Finally, however, at the poem's crucial point of contact with the classical tradition, Freneau chose as his central metaphor the elm tree, with its inescapable connotations of death. Although his is a "sweet," "lovely," and "shady" elm, it is one tightly linked to the western sense of the transience of human life. It is not impossible, in other words, that in "The Dying Elm" Freneau's overriding sense of his own best lyric instincts was that they swung unerringly toward the subject of death. Man's inevitable frustration as a result of trying to merge with the benign harmonies of nature is argued in almost every lyric poem Freneau published up to the time of "The Dying Elm." The solution he offers to this frustration in "The Farmer's Winter Evening" and "The House of Night" is death itself. Death stands between human beings and a (hopefully) satisfying reunion with physical nature. Although "The Dying Elm," like "Santa Cruz," evokes a mood of pastoral longing, of wanting to commune with nature, it too implies, in the emblem of the elm, that the only avenue to such a communion may be death.

"The Dying Elm" is unique among the poems Freneau published before 1780. The compressed, covert, and intensely private style sets it off from all the other lyrics he had published to date and suggests that Freneau wrote the first draft of this poem considerably later than the first drafts of the other poems, perhaps as late as summer 1779. Yet its tone and theme remain sentimental, wistful, romantic. As in "The American Village," "The Farmer's Winter Evening," and "Santa Cruz," there is a yearning for escape from harsh realities and an invocation of the tender impulses of human beings and nature. The poem appears to argue that agreeable, positive poetry is better than disagreeable, negative poetry and that the best inspiration for the preferred kind is nature in its benign aspects. Although ruined in natural fact, Freneau's favorite isle still beckoned in fancy.

III

"Learn What It Is
to Go to Sea," 1780-1786

In 1778 Robert Bell published and gave Freneau a complimentary copy of the fourth number of the *Miscellanies for
Sentimentalists* series, which included Freneau's patriotic poem
"American Independence." In this volume, which he kept for
the rest of his life, Freneau scribbled marginalia from time to
time. The most interesting of the marginalia appear in the section titled "Maxims and Moral Reflections by the Duke de la
Rochefoucault." On the back of the dedication page for the
section, Freneau penned three maxims of his own, the first
two bearing no resemblance to any of the hundreds that followed in Rochefoucault's list. Wrote Freneau: "The good conceal from Men the happiness of Death that they may endure
life. The world is undone by looking at things at a distance. A
man who finds not satisfaction in himself looks for it in vain
elsewhere."[1] The first and last of these aphorisms, taken together, imply that the wise conceal important truths from
others and learn to draw purely private satisfaction from them.
The second aphorism, startling and enigmatic though it is, is
linked to the other two in the sense that when people detach
themselves from conventional ways of viewing things, as the

first and third maxims recommend, they cut themselves off from those who cling to the conventional. Together, the aphorisms reveal that sometime after 1778 Freneau wrote a note to himself approving the masking of serious private thought and the seeking of personal satisfactions entirely apart from other human beings.

How soon after 1778 did he write them? Although the maxims are in Freneau's "earlier" handwriting, this only proves that they were penned before the second decade of the nineteenth century. "The Dying Elm" suggests that by June 1779 he had begun to develop the covert style that marked his best subsequent work. Possibly "The Dying Elm" emerged from a period of intense thought either inspired by or concurrent with Bell's gift and reflected in the Rochefoucault marginalia. Certainly the difference in technique between "The Dying Elm" and all of Freneau's previously published works, except for the essentially far different island passage in "The American Village" and the conclusion of "The Farmer's Winter Evening," suggests some such artistic revolution. It is probably safe to view the marginalia as evidence not of a specific change of mind at a specific time but of a general intellectual set that underlay Freneau's most serious work for the next decade.

There was one specific event, however, that seems to have had direct and permanent influence on Freneau's post-1780 philosophy. This was his capture by the British from the brig *Aurora* and his subsequent six-week incarceration on the prison ships *Scorpion* and *Hunter* during June and July 1780. Freneau scholars agree that this was probably the most scarring experience of his life, permanently filling him with hatred for England.[2] The resulting poem, *The British Prison Ship*, was, despite its artificial epic patina, among the most bitter he ever wrote. First published in spring 1781 in broadside with the 1780 poem "On the Death of Capt. N. Biddle," it chronicles Freneau's embarkation from Philadelphia on the blockade runner *Aurora* in late May, his capture by the British off the New Jersey coast the next day, and his subsequent miseries aboard the two prison ships anchored in New York harbor. Showing little sign of symbolic or metaphorical complexity, the poem offers a fast-paced narrative designed to enrage readers against the British. It ends with a call to destroy every Englishman in America.[3]

On the *Scorpion* and *Hunter*, Freneau for the first time personally saw and felt "man's inhumanity to man." Earlier, as "The Dying Elm" hints, he felt he was merely playing a somewhat distasteful and coarsening role as poet-agitator and propagandist. As a result of his incarceration, he seems to have thrown off for good his youthful idealism and romanticism. Although *The British Prison Ship* reveals no remarkable difference in tone or manner from his earlier propagandistic poems, it nevertheless represents a clear line of demarcation in Freneau's artistic career. After 1780 he begins to explore in depth the grim symbolic potential of the sea rather than simply to oppose it, as he did in "The American Village," with an ideal he knows he can never realize. The shock of those weeks in prison seems finally to have freed him from what had in any case become an untenable intellectual position. For the next six years, through the publication of his first major collection in 1786, his best poems, though often bitter and angry, direct their bitterness and anger more against his earlier romanticism than against the potential delusiveness of nature. They are more reactions against his philosophical past than resolutions of the new philosophical problems they raise. Sharply rejecting the romantic fancy of earlier poems like "The American Village," "Santa Cruz," and "The House of Night," they smolder with a harsh, skeptical empiricism that would have stunned Witherspoon had he recognized its debt to his own Common-Sense teachings. The poems recommend a selfish, stoic indifference to life that in the long run proved to be as unworkable a personal philosophy for Freneau as the romantic escapism he indulged in during the seventies.

With the publication of *The British Prison Ship*, the ocean and those who sail it become major subjects of his verse. The first poem he published after the *Prison Ship* broadside was his celebrated "Poem on the memorable victory obtained by the gallant capt. Paul Jones, of the Good Man Richard, over the Seraphis, etc. under the command of capt. Pearson," which appeared in the August 8, 1781, issue of Bailey's just-founded *Freeman's Journal*. "The Memorable Victory" is a ruggedly balladic narrative of Jones's incredible triumph over a superior British fleet on the night of September 23, 1779, off the east coast of England. Its last fifteen stanzas repeatedly evoke the horror of submersion in the ocean. Stanza 11 introduces the theme with the phrase "greedy waves" (1. 63), which is reinforced by the rhetorical question in stanza 12 asking whether Jones had died and "sunk to Neptune's caves below" (1.69) and the similarly rhetorical question in stanza 13 regarding how many of Jones's crew are "clasp'd in ocean's dark embrace" (1. 75). Stanza 16 asserts that many of Pearson's crew "were bury'd in the main" (1. 96); stanzas 18 and 19 bring the theme to a climax by reversing the poem's many allusions to the flow of blood outward from wounds as the mark of human vulnerability and portraying the *Good Man Richard* as a person whose wounds let death *in*:

> *Fatal to her, the ocean brine*
> *Pour'd thro' each spacious wound;*
> *Quick in the deep she disappear'd.* . . .
> (11. 110-12)

That Freneau should associate the ocean with death and destruction is not surprising, given his earlier treatment of it in "The American Village," "The Beauties of Santa Cruz," and "Columbus to Ferdinand." What is new here is glorification of a man whom the poem presents as the incarnation of that destructiveness. Achilleslike, Jones is transfigured at the height of battle, "Fierce lightnings blazing in his face" (1. 78). Despite Freneau's deprecation of the battle's carnage in the tenth and eighteenth stanzas, he hails Jones at the end with the epithet "great man" (1. 115) and urges him to continue scourging the British. At the very least, "The Memorable Victory" equates Jones's ruthlessness with that of the sea and freely grants its usefulness in America's pursuit of victory. Jones is a butcher, but the goal of beating the British justifies almost any means.

This ruthless tone, absent from Freneau's propagandistic verse before 1780, saturates his poetry in the early eighties. Sure of having all his work published by *The Freeman's Journal*, Freneau in fall 1781 gave the icy hatred of Britain born on the *Scorpion* and *Hunter* free rein in a series of merciless satires and cries for vengeance against Cornwallis, ending his crow of triumph at Cornwallis's Yorktown defeat, for example, with lines so brutal and vindictive that he removed or completely changed most of them in all the editions after 1786.[4] He similarly anathematized Benedict Arnold in *The Freeman's Journal* of July 10, 1781, in "The tenth ode of Horace's Book of Epodes, imitated" and lashed out against Tory loyalists and all Englishmen involved in the American war in dozens of poems published up to the end of 1783.

Although the nonpolitical, nonpropagandistic poems Freneau published during this same period were relatively few, they translated into private, nonpolitical terms the vein of harsh realism found in the public verse. "A Moral Thought," later retitled "The Vanity of Existence," appeared in fall 1781. Despite the didactic and morally conventional opening of stanzas 1 and 2, the poem concludes with a starkly realistic ocean image. And, though conventional, the two stanzas, arguing that the idealism of youth inevitably crumbles before the realities of adult experience, seem to summarize what had happened to Freneau since 1779. The final two stanzas offer an arresting analogy for this process of disillusionment.

> So nightly on the flowing tide,
>   Oft have I seen a raree-show;
> Reflected stars on either side,
>   And glittering moons were seen below.
>
> But when the tide had ebb'd away,
>   The scene fantastic with it fled,
> A bank of mud around me lay,
>   And sea-weed on the river's bed.[5]

The seaweed-strewn mud bank controls the poem, conveying the speaker's disgust not only at the deluded naiveté of belief in the glittering surface but, simultaneously, at the slimy reality below. The image expresses resentment toward both the deception and the truth. Yet the resentment is controlled. Freneau has chosen a setting that lets him view an ocean phenomenon, the tide, from land and bring the land and sea together in the form of a tidal river. The final line underscores the conflict between the speaker's land-based point of view and the vast power that produces tides even in freshwater rivers: lying on "the river's bed" is "sea-weed" thrust inland from the ocean, suggesting even more awesome realities offshore. Although Freneau pictures the sea here in traditional preromantic terms as a place of confusion, danger, and disillusionment, he also suggests that only fools can ignore its lessons.

Thus despite its superficial tone, "A Moral Thought" accurately sketches Freneau's intellectual position in the early 1780s. Like the speaker of the poem, he remains basically a landsman, despite his knowledge of what figuratively and literally lies beneath the tidal waters. He, too, feels the disappointment and even outrage of the landsman whose pastoral daydreams — "Life's flow'ry fields" (1. 3), as he calls them in the

poem's opening stanza—vanish with the tide, leaving the har-
bingers of ocean reality strewn behind. Yet disillusionment is
not only inevitable, he implies, but desirable. We must face
empirical truth, no matter how bitter, squarely.

A further attack on humankind's tendency to avoid truth
and cling to illusion appeared several months after "A Moral
Thought" in *The Freeman's Journal* of January 2, 1782, under
the title "Plato the Philosopher to his friend Theon." In this
eighty-eight-line poem, Freneau repeats, with embellishments,
the argument of the first two stanzas of "A Moral Thought"
by having Plato instruct an old man named Theon, a character
Freneau has invented, on the need to prepare himself for death.
The tactfulness of such a harangue, which Theon has apparently not requested, doubtful enough in the *Freeman's Journal*
version, is further called into question by the 1795 edition, in
which Freneau abandons the Plato-Theon fiction and simply
titles the poem "To an Old Man." Less pretentious and more
honest though the the revised title is, since Freneau's real purpose in the early version was obviously the same as in 1795,
the poem smacks even more of the arrogance of a young man
(Freneau was not yet thirty when the poem first appeared)
lecturing an old man on how to die. Like "A Moral Thought,"
it is a veiled statement of personal belief, this time almost bel-
ligerent in tone.

Stanza 5 strikes the note heard throughout.

> *Constrain'd to dwell with pain and care;*
> *These dregs of life are bought too dear,*
> *'Tis better far to die than bear*
> *The torments of another year.*[6]

Imagined as being spoken to an old man, as the poem requires,
the lines seem extraordinarily callous. Freneau's contempt for
what he sees as a desperate hanging on to life in Theonlike,
old people is equally clear in the fifteenth stanza, in which he

scornfully dismisses the "grandeur of this earthly round / Where Theon would forever be" (11. 57-58). Yet the poem is obviously aimed not only at reluctant senior-citizen candidates for the cemetery. It attacks all who refuse to ponder and accept the fact of their own death and the transience of all natural things. That Freneau is troubled, as in "A Moral Thought," not only by humankind's general blindness to this fact but by the fact itself is suggested in the sixteenth stanza, where, in the poem's most dramatic moment, the speaker bursts out,

> *Give me the stars, give me the skies,*
> *Give me the heaven's remotest sphere,*
> *Above these gloomy scenes to rise*
> *Of desolation and despair.*
>
> (11. 61-64)

To what extent the lines express Freneau's genuine emotion and to what extent they are a device to introduce the quasi-Platonic argument of the poem's final four stanzas is hard to judge. As in "A Moral Thought," Freneau seems personally involved in what his speaker is saying yet at the same time detached enough to make it sound rather staged. In any case, the poem ends with Plato's advice to Theon to forget this world and aspire "Where plants of life the plains invest / and green eternal crowns the year" (11. 77-78). As Adkins has shown,[7] Freneau's convictions concerning life after death are all but impossible to puzzle out from his writings. Many of his poems seem to deny personal immortality; others, like "Plato to Theon," seem to affirm some form of it. The ambiguity is evident in "A Moral Thought," whose conventional first half ends with the assertion that "Death is to wake to rise again, / To that true life I best esteem" (11. 7-8). Reaching an immortality "I best esteem" sounds too casual to be convincing—somewhat like being urged to worship a god the speaker neglects to identify. It seems most sensible to conclude that although Freneau considered immortality—whether quasi-Platonic, as in this poem, Christian, or in some other form—possible, he saw death as the one certainty every human being could depend on. It is this idea that seems to be uppermost in the final stanza of "Plato to Theon."

> *Life's journey past, for death prepare,*
> *Tis but the freedom of the mind,*
> *Jove made us mortal—his we are,*
> *To Jove dear Theon be resign'd.*
>
> (11. 85-88)

To argue that death means "freedom of the mind," as a Platonist presumably would, is to suggest possibilities that include a total cessation of thought—"freedom," that is, from the contradictions and confusions that a sensitive person necessarily perceives, as the entire poem has argued, in human existence. Further, the stanza expresses the stoic, radically anti-Platonic idea that the best preparation for death is to be "resigned" to the inexplicable forces that create and govern life. However one prepares for death, prepare for it one must, for it will surely come.

Aside from the half-humorous "Stanzas Occasioned by the Ruins of a Country Inn," which appeared three weeks after "Plato to Theon," and "On a Lady's Singing Bird," printed six months later, Freneau published no nonpolitical verse, except New Year's poems, until March 1784. On the seventeenth of that month, however, *The Freeman's Journal* carried "The Dying Indian; or Last Words of Shalum." An irregular ode of sixty-eight lines, "The Dying Indian" reveals more clearly than any of the poems Freneau had published since 1780 the negative, skeptical drift of his thought concerning life after death during the period. In the poem a sympathetic speaker, Shalum, free of classical or Christian influence, speculates on what lies beyond death and then dies. Although Freneau sets Shalum's speculations in the framework of the Indian myth of the happy hunting ground, he portrays him throughout as "Perplext with doubts, and tortur'd with despair."[8] Shalum's problem is that although he pictures death as at worst a dreamlike state in which he will have some measure of existence, he fears it will not offer paradiselike forests full of game but "empty unsubstantial shades" (1. 16) of forests crossed by "Lazy and sad deluding waters" (1. 26)—in other words, "emptier groves" (1. 37) than those he has known in life.

Freneau is using Shalum as a mouthpiece to express his own doubts and perplexities about what death will bring. Like Shalum, he is questioning the prevalent death mythology of his culture and suggesting that the Christian promise of eternal life may be empty—"who can shew," queries Shalum, "that half the tale is true" (1. 33)? The conclusion of the poem strongly hints, in fact, that to die is to be annihilated. The final two lines are spoken by an omniscient narrator who for the first time intrudes:

> He spoke, and bid the attending mourners weep;
> Then clos'd his eyes, and sunk to endless sleep.
>
> (11. 67-68)

Although "endless sleep" might be read merely as a poetic euphemism for death, in the context both of the poem and of Freneau's intense contemplation of death during this period, it seems to carry a significance beyond that of mere variation. Placed as the poem's last words and spoken not by Shalum but by the poem's controlling intelligence, it tends to confirm Shalum's worst fears: death is to life as sleeping is to waking. "Endless sleep" also undercuts Shalum's final speculation. Just before he dies he expresses the hope that

> Nature at least these ruins may repair,
> When death's long dream is o'er, & she forgets to weep;

Some real world once more may be assign'd,
Some new born mansion for the immortal mind! —

(11. 54-57)

If, as the narrator asserts, the sleep of death is "endless," Shalum's hope is patently vain.

Although one of Freneau's most pessimistic poems on death, "The Dying Indian" expresses an ultimate-voyage, final-adventure view of dying that he returned to in several subsequently published poems. Shalum says that "Relentless demons urge" him "to that shore, / On whose bleak forests all the dead are cast: . . . where all is strange, and all is new. . . ." (11. 3-4 and 7). His last command is to put

My trusty bow, and arrows by my side,
The cheerful bottle and the ven'son store;
For long the journey is that I must go,
Without a partner, and without a guide.

(11. 63-66)

Although he sounds less than eager for the trip, he gets his weapons and supplies ready in true Indian fashion for the most demanding expedition of all. The fact he goes alone, "without a guide," links the poem to several of Freneau's sea poems on death, in which the lack of pilots to navigate the ocean of death symbolizes how totally unknown its waters are to all living people.

In sum, the scars of Freneau's prison-ship experience in 1780 are visible in the poetry he published during the next four years in several ways. First, the savagery of the political verse he aimed at the then thoroughly hated British indicates a new determination to confront unpleasant realities — realities of the kind he apparently tried to avoid when he sailed for the Caribbean in 1776. Second, his preoccupation with death in the handful of nonpolitical poems he wrote suggests that his prison-ship experience deepened and sobered his private thought by thrusting the fact of death and mortal anguish upon him in a way he had never before felt. Finally, the new insistence, audible in the post-*Prison Ship* poems, that life be viewed with a coldly empirical eye free of illusion and shallow optimism marks the end of his youthful longings for a pastoral ideal.

As already suggested, however, he did not abandon pastoralism. Instead, he increasingly used it as a vehicle for propaganda and, more complexly, as what he believed to be a valuable social and political goal for the new nation. Although privately he relegated pastoralism to the recreational status evident in the 1779 version of "Santa Cruz," publicly he set higher value than ever on a sort of prototypical Jeffersonian agrarianism as America's answer to European corruption. Many of the political poems he wrote between 1780 and 1784 evoke an image of the free and independent American shepherd-farmer, morally uplifted by contact with nature and fiercely jealous of the rights nature has given him. This image underlies his finest elegiac piece, "To the memory of the brave Americans, under general Greene, who fell in the action of Sept. 8, 1781," which appeared in *The Freeman's Journal* two months after the battle. The Americans who died in the fighting are pictured as heroic swains who left their fields to defend themselves against brutal invaders, and much of the poem's force stems from Freneau's subtly contrasting the harmony of the "rural reign"[9] of the American "shepherds" (1. 12) then and the deserted battlefield now with the violence of the battle itself. By implication, the "rural reign" has been restored in the poem's present, and the mourner to whom the poem is addressed is defined as a sympathetic shepherd. He is asked to perform a series of gestures of grief so classically stylized and formal that the allusions to shepherds, spears and shields, and Parthian battle strategy seem part of a ritual resembling a choric response from Greek drama. The speaker asks the mourner to "smite" his "gentle breast" (1. 7), to "sigh" (11. 11 and 12), and to "adorn" the shepherds' "humble graves" (1. 13). Freneau's call for a pastoral dignity and simplicity of grief on the part of the shepherd-mourner—and by extension every American—reinforces the pastoral connotations with which he surrounds the American warriors, making it seem as though, too innocent for the vicious enemy they faced, they had thrown themselves on their enemies' weapons like brave children.

Eight months later, in July 1782, *The Freeman's Journal* published a less sophisticated example of Freneau's revised pastoralism. "Philosophical Reflections," a seventy-eight-line verse essay in heroic couplets, is Freneau's first poetic venture into the popular primitivism of the day. It sets forth a glib and simplistic theory of moral decay since "that age of innocence and ease / When men, yet social, knew no ills"[10] like those of modern war and monarchy. In true primitivist fashion, Freneau leaves this happy time altogether vague in terms of time and place, asserting simply that the "hoary sage beneath his sylvan shade, / Impos'd no laws but those which reason made; / On peace not war, on good not ill intent, / He judg'd his brethren by their own consent. . . ." (11. 33-36). Not only was this patriarch of "some small tribe . . . In virtue firm, and obstinately just," but he "knew no murder and he felt no fear" (11. 38 and 44). Freneau explains the subsequent slide from these virtues into modern despotism as the result of "Ambition" (1. 61), which "tempts the weak mind, and leads the heart astray" (1. 68). Although he was unquestionably sincere in his dislike of despotism and the personal ambition that he believed caused it, Freneau was no more a genuine primitivist in 1782 than in 1772, when he in effect privately disavowed primitivism in "The American Village." His lack of sympathy in the early and middle eighties with golden-age primitivism is shown by a poem published in 1785 and titled "The Five Ages," which ridicules primitivist doctrine in galloping anapests, tracing the deterioration of humankind through the classical era of gold, silver, and brass to the modern age of iron, and satirically, a possible future age of paper. His tone is plain in stanza 4:

> *Yet some say there never was seen on this stage,*
> *What poets affirm of that innocent age,*
> *When the brutal creation from bondage was free,*
> *And men were exactly what mankind should be.*[11]

He concludes good-humoredly that the present age, imperfect as it is, will do.

> *So, it's best, I believe, that things are as they are.*
> *If iron's the meanest—we've nothing to fear.*
> (11.51-52)

He used primitivism in propagandistic poems like "Philosophical Reflections" after 1780 because it was a useful device, familiar to his readers, for distinguishing virtuous Americans from decadent Europeans and for interpreting history in a way congenial to the rural and provincial prejudices of the rebelling colonies.

Freneau's interest in the literary possibilities of primitivism during this period is also apparent in the series of nineteen prose essays he contributed to *The Freeman's Journal* between November 1781 and August 1782 under the guise of the Pilgrim, a fifty-six-year-old Swiss bachelor so saturated with primitivist ideology that he lives in a secret cave in the wilderness outside Philadelphia. Much of his depiction of the Pilgrim's love of rural simplicity is tongue-in-cheek, and, as Philip Marsh has pointed out, Freneau's interest in the Pilgrim's primitivism flags after the first few essays and gives way to a concern for modern urban and political affairs.[12] Yet the Pilgrim gives Freneau a point from which to attack the vices of modern civilization and to argue that Americans should keep their civilization free of the pomp and clutter of Europe. Furthermore, the

Pilgrim essays, though always aimed at a newspaper audience presumably oblivious to symbols, at points give hints of Freneau's deeper private thought. One of the most interesting instances of this sort of sudden illumination occurs in essay XII, which warns against the danger of too much academic learning and recommends useful occupations like farming and the mechanical trades over the learned professions. "The illiterate man of invention," casually remarks the Pilgrim,

> is a Columbus, who, born to rely upon himself, boldly launches out into the immense ocean of ideas, and brings to light new worlds teeming with gold and diamonds, before unknown;—the scholar is the timorous and cautious pilot, who creeping along shores already discovered, by the help of his lead and line, makes shift, in a bungling manner, to get from port to port; or, if he at last attempts the main ocean, it is in the track of him that first explored the way.[13]

As the passage shows, the ocean connoted to Freneau mental venturesomeness of all kinds, which of course included the daring of Columbus portrayed earlier in "Columbus to Ferdinand." The ocean was already rich with meaning for him by 1784, when he decided to try making a living on it, and for the next six years he drew from it extraordinary inspiration.

The first poetic fruits of his going to sea professionally were the superb "Verses, made at Sea, in a Heavy Gale," published April 13, 1785, in *The Freeman's Journal* and retitled "The Hurricane" in the 1795 *Poems*. From the first of its thirty-six lines to the last, "The Hurricane" strikes a symbolic resonance unmatched in any of Freneau's earlier poems. The first two stanzas contrast the peril of the ship's crew caught in the hurricane with the relative safety of other creatures, human and animal, on land.

> *Happy the man who, safe on shore,*
> *Now trims, at home, his evening fire;*

> *Unmov'd he hears the tempest roar,*
> *That on the tufted groves expire:*
> *Alas! on us they doubly fall,*
> *Our feeble barque must bear them all.*

> *Now to their haunts, the birds retreat,*
> *The squirrel seeks his hollow tree,*
> *Wolves in their shaded caverns meet,*
> *All, all are blest but wretched we—*
> *Foredoom'd a stranger to repose,*
> *No rest the unsettled ocean knows.*[14]

Although the land is relatively secure, it serves merely as a buffer to the storm—as a refuge and haven—and not as a truly counterbalancing force. The fact that the winds fall "doubly" hard on the ship implies they carry their message inland as well, although the landsman hears them "unmov'd." His being "Happy" in his disregard of what is happening on the open sea suggests imperceptiveness, and the assertion that he and other land creatures are "blest" further hints of their blissful ignorance of the appalling reality offshore.

The symbolic meaning of this reality is clarified in the next two stanzas.

> *While o'er the dark abyss we roam,*
> *Perhaps, whate'er the pilots say,*
> *We saw the Sun descend in gloom,*
> *No more to see his rising ray,*
> *But bury'd low, by far too deep,*
> *On coral beds, unpitied, sleep!*

> *But what a strange, uncoasted strand,*
> *Is that, where death permits no day—*
> *No charts have we to mark that land,*
> *No compass to direct that way—*

What pilot shall explore that realm,
What new Columbus take the helm!
(ll. 13-24)

The verb "sleep!" at the end of the first stanza can have either "We" or "Sun" in the third line as its subject. If the subject is "We," the sense of the stanza is simply that we, the sailors, may drown and lie unpitied on the coral beds. If, however, it is "Sun," the stanza's meaning radically widens to include the sun itself as a potential victim of the storm. Syntactic ambiguity is a device Freneau uses here and in a number of his best poems to mask disturbing meanings from unwary readers. He is inviting us to see the hurricane as a symbol of the chaotic and destructive forces in nature and, further, as conceivably capable of swallowing up nature's benign forces, here epitomized by the sun, in some stupendous, cosmic cataclysm. The implied disagreement with the "pilots" in the second line is a disagreement with the religious and philosophical optimists who affirm nature's stability and benevolence. In addition Freneau may be making an irreverent pun on the word "Sun" and implying that in a natural universe thought of as a hurricane the Christian Son would also drown and most certainly have no "rising ray."

The central meaning of the "dark abyss," as Freneau points out in line 20, is "death"—that "strange uncoasted strand" at the bottom of the ocean of nature where not merely sailors lie drowned but the sun may be ultimately extinguished. The ocean that in "The American Village" symbolizes general destructiveness is here specifically linked to human mortality. The sailors on their coral beds will be "unpitied" by all those who, like the landsman mentioned in the opening stanzas, have never faced up to the elemental sea. Freneau is saying, metaphorically, that to confront the elemental sea—to go through a hurricane—is to learn not only that nature in its ocean aspect is not benign but that dying may mean being swallowed up in the hurricane of an utterly chaotic and meaningless universe.[15] The ocean here, suggesting death without immortality as well as natural chaos, represents a vision utterly foreign to the landsman, who in contrast to the poem's speaker is shielded from this nihilistic hurricane by the "tufted groves" of an apparently benign natural universe and, through implication, by belief in his own immortality. As in "The Dying Indian," Freneau here stresses that there are "No charts," "No compass," and no Columbuslike "pilot" to show the way through this weird undersea of death. But though Shalum looks forward, however hesitantly, to death as the final exploratory adventure, the speaker of "The Hurricane" darkly hints it will be no adventure at all but annihilation. In this respect, "The Hurricane" confirms the bleak reading already offered for the omniscient speaker's "endless sleep" remark at the end of "The Dying Indian."

The concluding stanzas of the poem underline the hurricane's random violence.

> *While death and darkness both surround,*
> *And tempests rage with lawless power,*
> *Of friendship's voice, I hear no sound,*
> *No comfort in this dreadful hour—*
>   *What friendships can in tempests be,*
>   *What comfort on this angry sea?*
>
> *The barque, accustom'd to obey,*
> *No more the trembling pilots guide,*
> *Alone she gropes her trackless way,*
> *While mountains burst on either side—*
>   *Thus, skill and science both must fall,*
>   *And ruin is the lot of all.*
>
> (11.25-36)

The final two lines, like the poem as a whole, are tentative. On one hand, they imply that if the hurricane is ultimate reality then nature is at the core sheer chaos. On the other, they can be read as saying that the hurricane is merely one of nature's manifestations and that a land-oriented, pastoral vision of natural harmony and order may be an equally valid — or invalid — interpretation of the physical universe. In any case, there is little question that in these final stanzas the hurricane emerges as an uncompromisingly harsh symbol of the meaninglessness of individual death. The friendship and sociability Freneau associates with land vanish during "this dreadful hour": as a metaphor for personal dissolution, the "angry sea" offers little hope for survival in a future life — no immortal "friendships" or "comfort" — and implies instead that to die is at best to enter the "lawless" chaos of the elements. One of the poem's most appalling images is that of "mountains burst[ing] on either side," which not only captures the fury of the storm but suggests total collapse of those land features that in subsequent poems Freneau used to suggest the utmost solidity nature could offer and that here undercut the supposed security of the landsman "safe on shore."

The tentativeness of its conclusion about nature's inner meaning notwithstanding, "The Hurricane" is, like "The Dying Indian," a stern, dark poem. That Freneau was intensely pondering death in 1784 and 1785 is suggested by the number of poems dealing with the subject that he published during the period. At least half of the dozen poems he printed between "The Dying Indian" in March 1784 and the end of 1785 were either elegiac in tone or, like "The Hurricane," centrally concerned with some aspect of death. Two of these, "The Deserted Farm House" and "The Monument of Phaon," are unusually revealing in different ways. "The Deserted Farm House," which appeared in *The Freeman's Journal* a month after "The Hurricane," was an unsmiling revision of the mock-pastoral "Upon a Very Ancient Dutch House on Long-Island" that had been included in the 1772 "American Village" volume. Although the earlier version pokes fun at the Dutch and their pipe-smoking, hefty women, the revision omits all national-cultural particulars about the farmhouse's inhabitants and soberly universalizes the fate of the farmhouse in two new stanzas. It beomes an emblem of the transience of human civilization. Like Rome and Joppa, it cannot survive the ravages of time.[16]

"The Monument of Phaon," appearing a week later in *The Freeman's Journal*, is a narrative of two deaths by water. Based on Ovid's tale of the poet Sappho's love for the fabulously handsome Phaon, the poem invents a meeting between Sappho and a traveler just back from Sicily who recites to her an epitaph he saw on a tombsone erected there to Phaon by a Sicilian woman named Musidora. Musidora, Phaon's lover, tells how he died after drinking water from an ice-cold spring on a hot, summer day. When Sappho hears about the death she upbraids Phaon for betraying her and leaps from a cliff into the ocean in hopes of being reunited with him in the underworld. Interpreting the poem is complicated by the fact that although Freneau indicated no date of composition in *The Freeman's Journal* version, he claimed a year later in the 1786 *Poems* that it was written in 1770. Perhaps a version of it was written then, like the "Ancient Dutch House," but the central themes of "The Monument to Phaon" are so similar to those of Freneau's most serious work in the mideighties that significant revision, if not first composition, is suggested during the later period. At the poem's climax, the speaker kills herself by leaping into the ocean. More significant, the poem introduces the wanderer theme that dominates a number of important, later poems. The idea least consistent with Freneau's mature thought is Phaon's death after drinking fresh water, and it was perhaps this inconsistency that led him to omit the entire epitaph section, containing more that two-thirds of the poem's original lines, from the 1795 version. There, no allusion is made to the way Phaon died: the poem consists simply of the traveler's telling

Sappho that Phaon is dead and of her throwing herself into the sea.[17]

The darkness of Freneau's thought at this time is further suggested by a poem he published February 2, 1786, in the Charleston, South Carolina, *Columbian Herald*. "Lines written at the Pallisades, near Port-Royal, in the Island of Jamaica— September 1784" describes the town of Port Royal, destroyed by tidal wave in 1692 and still almost uninhabited in Freneau's day. For the first time since "Santa Cruz," Freneau returns to the symbolic relationship between destructive ocean and benign land that he introduced fifteen years earlier in the island passage in "The American Village." Before the catastrophe, Port Royal was the "glory"[18] of Jamaica. But as the speaker walks through its ruins he visualizes "Past scenes of death" (1. 16), in which "the dark ocean roll'd across the land" (1. 18), crushing the city and drowning hundreds of its denizens. What remains after nearly a hundred years, the speaker continues, is a "spit of sand" (1. 33) and "mouldering mounds that scarce oppose the sea" (1. 34). This is a symbolic deluge and erosion: the sea devours the land as death devours the living.

After contemptuously describing the remains of humanity living in Port Royal in the poem's present—its worn-out slaves and political outlaws—the speaker rebukes himself for visiting the place, since it has filled him with bitterness and despair. "Where shall I go," he bursts out,

> *what* Lethe *shall I find,*
> *To drink these dark ideas from my mind!*
> (11. 49-50)

Among the most poignant Freneau wrote, the lines reveal a depth of spiritual anguish not commonly associated with his poetry, yet unmistakably charted in the major poems of this period. Although echoing the allusion to Lethe at the end of the 1772 "Farmer's Winter Evening," the lines treat Lethean oblivion not as a means to a supernal loveliness that may be but as a simple blotting out of the ugliness that is. In this version the poem ends with eight lines of sarcastic description, which immediately follow the outburst but which Freneau amplified for the 1788 *Works* into one of his grimmest and most complex repudiations of hope, as we shall see.

That there was a deep conflict in Freneau's mind is apparent in most of the lyrics he published between 1780 and early 1786. On one hand is his willingess to face death realistically and to concede the possibility it was the sole end of all existence; on the other, his revulsion against such a bleak world view. The last poem he committed to the newspapers before the 1786 *Poems* appeared reveals this ambivalence plainly. "The Lost Adventurer," a sixty-line account of an old sailor named Ralph that appeared in the *Columbian Herald* March 6, 1786, has been judged by Philbrick to be Freneau's most successful maritime poem.[19] Although based on a wholly nonsymbolic reading, Philbrick's assessment may not seem grossly inflated to those who find symbolic intricacies in the poem as well.

Intricate "The Lost Adventurer" certainly is. Besides touching on almost every land-sea idea raised in earlier poems, it establishes a more complex story line and adventurer-character than we have encountered before. Opening with a four-line introduction by an "I" narrator who is presumably Freneau, the poem then quotes Ralph, the "Lost Adventurer" of the title, who speaks until the final stanza, which the narrator delivers. The effect of this frame structure—used previously by Freneau only in "The Dying Indian", and there much more simply—is not merely to absolve the "I" narrator of responsibility for what Ralph says but to underline in the final stanza the disparity between Ralph's preaching and practice. By separating himself from Ralph's arguments, Freneau is able to express some of his own ambivalence by presenting it through

Ralph's confused and contradictory point of view. He is probably, in fact, through Ralph subtly mocking himself.

As the poem opens, the narrator finds Ralph on a tropical island mending sails. He is, like all sailors, a "slave of fortune"[20]— an archetypal ocean "Adventurer," as the title puts it. Ralph's first words explain why he originally went to sea: a ship seduced him.

> 'With masts so trim, and sails as white as snow,
> 'The painted barque allur'd me from the land,
> 'Pleas'd, on her sea-beat decks I wish'd to go
> 'Mingling my labours with her hardy band;
> 'The Captain bade me for the voyage prepare
> 'And said, by Jasus, 'tis a grand affair!
>
> (ll. 7-12)

It is revealing that Ralph pictures the lure of the sea in terms of a harlotlike ship. The only kind of femaleness Freneau ever associates with the sea is that of the prostitute or bold and amoral mistress or coquette. "Proper" women are always creatures of land who either oppose or encourage the male urge to wander but who themselves never go to sea. That Freneau felt some guilt over this seagoing urge in himself is suggested by the number of betrayed and abandoned women he sympathetically portrays in many other poems and here by his imaging of Ralph's going to sea as a yielding to seamy, sexual temptation. The ship is a whore who entices him from shore innocence by promising a life of reckless adventure. Even the Captain's boast that life at sea is a "grand affair" insinuates a similar meaning.

For the 1788 *Works*, Freneau inserted two new stanzas between the first and second of the *Columbian Herald* version which sharpen the poem's female land-male sea contrasts. In the new stanzas Ralph protests that originally he wanted to leave neither the land nor his girl "Amoranda":

Charm'd with the shallow stream, that murmur'd by,
I felt as blest as any swain could feel,
  Who, seeking nothing that the world admires,
  To one poor valley fix'd his whole desires.[21]

Ralph's self-analysis here recalls the whole course of Freneau's thought, from "The American Village" onward, concerning pastoral retreats where townspeople think shepherds and swains commune with nature. The "shallow stream," reminiscent of the island fountain of "The American Village," foreshadows Freneau's increasingly frequent use of similarly gentle, freshwater currents as symbolic contrasts to the bottomless sea. The currents' shallowness suggests lack of intellectual depth or excitement and yet, simultaneously, beneficence in poems after 1786. They are usually associated, as here, with women or domestic comforts for which the seagoing adventurer longs. Near them, as Ralph implies in the lines above, the seafarer hopes to recapture some measure of the life of blissful ignorance idealized in "The American Village," "seeking nothing that the world admires."

It becomes evident as "The Lost Adventurer" proceeds that Freneau wants us to see Ralph as a badly confused tar. The next two stanzas offer a thoroughly muddled series of ideas on why men leave land. Says Ralph:

'To combat with the winds who first essay'd,
'Had these gay groves his lightsome heart beguil'd,
'His heart attracted by the charming shade
'Had chang'd the deep sea for the woody wild,
'And slighted all the gain that Neptune yields
'For Damon's cottage, or Palemon's fields.

'His barque, the bearer of a feeble crew,
'How could he trust, when none had been to prove her—
'Courage might sink when lands and shores withdrew,
'And sickly whelps might spoil the best manoeuvre;

'But, fortitude — though woes and death await,
'Still views bright *skies and leaves the* dark *to fate.*

(11. 13-24)

The whimsical, conditional event imagined in the first stanza, that of the first ocean voyager discovering Ralph's idyllic island and, enchanted by it, deciding to give up voyaging, totally contradicts what Ralph has done. As if sensing this gap in logic, Ralph shifts at the beginning of the next stanza to the fear this hypothesized first sailor must have felt, only to contradict himself again by praising the sailor's — and by implication his own — "fortitude," which he defines as acknowledging only *"bright* skies" and leaving "the *dark* to fate."

Freneau seems to be mocking yet at the same time sympathizing with Ralph's tortured thoughts. Full honesty, from Freneau's point of view, requires a better understanding and acceptance of ocean realities than Ralph's. Yet Freneau admires Ralph's concept of fortitude, as the next three stanzas and many subsequent poems reveal. Ralph continues by explaining how "disheartening" (1. 31) it is to bear not merely the physical hardships of life at sea but, more trying and more to Freneau's point, its constant threat of death. At the end of Ralph's speech, Freneau seems in fact momentarily to break through the mask, giving Ralph lines that echo the tone of "The Hurricane":

'Tis folly all! — for who can truly tell
'What streams disturb the bosom of that main;
'What ugly fish in those dark climates dwell
'That feast on men. . . .

(11. 37-40)

This is the mysterious realm of death symbolized as the undersea in "The Hurricane" and the afterlife Shalum doubts in "The Dying Indian." It also suggests the potential for universal chaos associated with the sea in "The Hurricane" and, less powerfully, in "The American Village" and "Santa Cruz." Like Ralph, though at a deeper level of awareness, Freneau is a lost adventurer, uncertain how to deal with the appalling implications of his metaphysical speculations. The fact that he begins at about this time to express increasing respect for Ralph's doctrine of fortitude, though again at a deeper level, further suggests his sympathy with this old sea dog's plight.

Yet there is no question Ralph is more confused than Freneau. He contradicts himself blatantly in the advice he gives at the end of his harangue:

> '. . . then stay, my gentle swain,
> 'Bred in yon' happy shades — be happy there,
> 'And be these quiet groves thy only care.'
>
> (11. 40-42)

Freneau underlines the contradiction in the final stanza by finishing the story himself.

> So spoke poor Ralph, and with a smooth sea gale
> Fled from the magic of the inchanting shore;
> But, whether winds or waters did prevail,
> I saw the black ship ne'er returning more;
>   Though long I walked the margin of the main,
>   And long have look'd, and still must look in vain.
>
> (11. 43-48)

These lines support both a serious and a humorous reading of the poem. On the serious side, they imply that Ralph has met a violent death on the very ocean he warned others away from but could not himself resist. His sinister, seductive "black ship" has delivered him to that horrible, undersea obliteration, without hope of immortality, that preyed on Freneau's mind during the mideighties. On the lighter side, the lines complete Ralph's amusing intellectual gyrations, picturing him bolting from the "inchanting" island for good. Much of the poem's interest comes from this controlled ambivalence, this willingness simultaneously to sympathize with and to mock the ocean adventurer. Interesting too is the fact that the Freneau-narrator, like the one of "A Moral Thought," remains on shore, suggesting that at least a part of Freneau's personality remained committed to land. He could feel the emotional and intellectual pull of a nihilistic world view yet would not give in to it.

We are told in Francis Bailey's "Advertisement," dated June 1, 1786, at the beginning of *The Poems of Philip Freneau Written Chiefly during the Late War*, that Freneau had left the 111 poems comprising the volume in Bailey's hands "above a year ago, with permission to publish them whenever I thought proper."[22] Assuming this to be true, we can conclude that none of the volume's poems were written or revised later than May 1785 even though some of them appeared in *The Freeman's Journal* during summer and fall 1785. It is not so easy to establish the earlier limits of their composition dates. From the way they are arranged in the book, they appear to have been set in roughly the chronological order of composition, early poems first, later poems last. But in fact Freneau dated virtually all the poems that had been previously published by date of publication, not composition. Concerning when they were actually written he gives us little solid information. For a number of the pre-*Freeman's Journal* poems he apparently supplied composition dates, which Bailey printed above the appropriate pieces.

Many of these dates raise questions. For example, "The Monument of Phaon" carries the same date—1770—as "The Citizen's Resolve." "The Citizen's Resolve" is a drastically revised version of "The Farmer's Winter Evening," included in the 1772 "American Village" volume. It completely inverts the tone of the earlier poem, reducing it to a joke on the original speaker by transforming him into a poltroonish merchant who gives up his trade to live like a shepherd in the country, becomes bored with country life, and three months later returns to the city.[23] So too with "The Deserted Farm-House," which, though given no date, is a revised version of "Upon a Very Ancient Dutch House on Long Island," also included in the "American Village" volume. Here, as has already been indicated, the mock-pastoral tone of the original is reversed. The 1786 version universalizes the fate of the farmhouse, stripping it of Dutch connotations and equating it with the ruins of Rome and Joppa. In both cases Freneau drastically rewrote the poems sometime between first publication in 1772 and republication in 1786. A reasonable presumption, buttressed by revisions he made in the *U.S. Magazine* poems, is that he rewrote the poems shortly before giving them to Bailey for the 1786 edition.

Revisions of "The House of Night" and "Santa Cruz" are especially interesting if compared with "The Power of Fancy," first published in the 1786 *Poems* but apparently one of the few in the collection finished during the seventies. Regularly anthologized, the "Power of Fancy" has been generally—and rightly—interpreted as Freneau's youthful declaration of independence from earlier Lockeian theories of mechanical association and image-making.[24] The first twenty and final fourteen lines define fancy as a "bright, celestial flame"[25] and liken it to the creative force of God. In the poem's middle 120 lines fancy emerges as the activity of mind celebrated by the mid-century British poets—memory cut loose from its sense-experience moorings, splicing together previously unrelated data stored in the brain and creating images not found in nature. Although in the 1795 edition Freneau combined the first twenty and last fourteen lines virtually without change into a poem he titled "Ode to Fancy" and recast the middle 120 lines, heavily revised, as a separate poem titled "Fancy's Ramble,"[26] he need not have. The original everywhere applauds the romantic theory of fancy that dominated Freneau's pre-1780 lyrics.

In contrast, revisions of the "House of Night" and "Santa Cruz" reveal a radical shift from this pre-1780, romantic theory to a post-1780 view that fancy is delusive and untrustworthy. Obvious in the "House of Night" revisions is Freneau's post-1780 preference for commonsense rationalism. The 1786 version, nearly twice the length of the original, repeatedly explains surrealistic, disjointed events in the first version by giving a rationale for how they happened. One of the most striking cases occurs in stanzas 106-12 of the 1786 version, where Freneau explains how the speaker gets outside the House of Night just before Death dies. In the 1779 version, the speaker simply finds himself outside listening,[27] but in the revision Freneau carefully points out that he leaves the house and walks to a "far off wood"[28] from which he hears and sees Death's death throes inside the house. Since this would be physically impossible, Freneau inserts a new stanza, in brackets, accounting for the speaker's x-ray vision.

> *[For fancy gave to my enraptur'd soul*
> *An eagle's eye, with keenest glance to see,*
> *And Bade those distant sounds distinctly roll*
> *Which, waking, never had affected me.]*
>
> (11. 45-48)

Equally obvious is the revision's tendency away from the romantic idea that the fancy can intuit supernatural truths to the idea that fancy lies. The 1786 version includes the following 1779 stanza verbatim:

> *Stranger, believe the truth experience tells,*
> *Poetic dreams are of a finer cast*
> *Than those which o'er the sober brain diffus'd,*
> *Are but a repetition of some action past.*[29]

But immediately afterward Freneau added a new stanza to the 1786 version:

> *Fancy, I own thy power—when sunk in sleep*
> *Thou play'st thy wild delusive part so well*
> *You lift me into immortality,*
> *Depict new heavens, or draw the scenes of hell.*
>
> (11. 17-20)

Fancy has here, by the mideighties, become "wild" and "delusive." That Freneau saw reason as being more in conflict with fancy after 1780 than before is further shown by his revision of the first line of the stanza following the one just quoted. In 1779 the line read, "By some sad means the mind cannot recal [*sic*] "; in 1786 it was changed to, "By some sad means, when Reason holds no sway" (1. 21). This sharpening of difference between the two faculties is not surprising, given Freneau's increasingly unromantic view of life after 1780.

But the most remarkable new element in the 1786 "House of Night" is its tone of Christian moralism. Freneau's aim in the 1779 version was to create a nightmarish aura of psychological distortion—associations dislodged from their root sensations—the bizarre climax of which is the death of Death. This aim changes in the 1786 version to one of quasi-Christian moral instruction, introduced in a prose "Advertisement" prefacing the poem. Opening with the claim that the poem "is founded upon the authority of Scripture, inasmuch as these sacred books assert, that *the last enemy that shall be conquered is Death*," the "Advertisement" previews some of the homiletic episodes to follow and ends by praising the concluding stanzas, new in the 1786 version, as "reflexions on the impropriety of a too great attachment to the present life, and incentives to such moral virtue as may assist in conducting us to a better." This new note of moral uplift is apparent throughout Freneau's revisions. One revealing instance is the addition in the 1786 version of a fourteen-stanza section explaining the background of the 1779 "comely youth" of "port majestic," now named Cleon, and radically changing his relationship with Death from the way it was presented in 1779. In 1779 the narrator simply finds the Cleon character in Death's sick-chamber and then listens to him deliver a vituperative harangue against Death. In 1786, Cleon's role is greatly—and oddly—amplified. Not only does he urge the narrator to be kind to Death and tend to his every wish, arguing that "The bleeding Savior of a world un- done / Bade thy compassion rise toward thy foe" (11. 149-50), but he explains that Death has just killed his (Cleon's) lovely wife Aspasia, a fact we are supposed to see as making his solici- tude for Death's comfort more noble by contrast with Death's obscene self-pity. The narrator, who in the original version passively observes the Cleon-Death conversation, in the revi- sion takes part in the action. He gives Death water and medicine and walks him around the house in a series of comically gro- tesque stanzas (11. 221-32 and 249-56). Heightening the moralistic tone of the 1786 version are several new passages that underline the Black-Mass quality of Death's funeral. When the narrator reaches Death's cemetery, for example, he finds an evil church "rais'd by sinners hands": "wicked were their hearts," he exclaims, "for they refus'd / To aid the helpless orphan, when distrest, / The shivering, naked stranger they mis-us'd, / And banish'd from their doors the starving guest" (11. 478 and 491-94). Similar changes give the 1786 poem an orthodox Christian flavor, as when Cleon, painting the horrors of hell, gives Death a Calvinistic tongue-lashing:

> 'And oh that HE, who spread the universe,
> Would cast one pitying glance on thee below;
> Millions of years in torments thou might'st fry,
> But thy eternity!—who can conceive its woe!'
> (11.337-40)

One feels on the basis of passages like this that the poem's climax could have been a classic, deathbed conversion.

Edwin Cady has astutely observed that "mockery was Fre- neau's game in 'The [1786] House of Night.'"[30] There is no doubt that well before 1780 Freneau had abandoned Christianity. That the current of his thought in the eighties was not merely non-Christian but dangerously nihilistic is demonstrated by poems like "The Dying Indian" and "The Hurricane." Read as satire, the 1786 "House of Night" burlesques Christian eschatology by reducing the death of Death to a lurid farce on the banks of Chesapeake Bay. Given virtually everything else Freneau was currently publishing and given the poem's mishmash of gothic grotesquerie, humor, moral sententiousness, rationalized surrealism, and Christian doctrine, it is impossible not to agree with Cady that Freneau's real intention was the opposite of the one set forth in the "Advertisement." His private aim, that is, seems to have been to ridicule what he saw by the mideighties as the complacent and uncritical acceptance by the vast majority of his contemporaries of the Christian myth of death. That he rewrote the poem "seriously" enough, giving it a strong homiletic and doctrinal flavor, to keep this incendiary aim hidden for 200 years is consistent with the method in all his best work. "The House of Night" is not a symbolic poem; its subtleties are of a different kind.

Freneau's butchering of the poem for the 1795 edition is explicable on these grounds. Having come round to a more affirmative philosophy by that time, he may have seen his earlier mockery, however surreptitious, as immature, cheaply cynical, and even unpatriotic—unpatriotic in the sense that it questioned a belief held by his countrymen and could, if perceived, lead to a weakening of the American social order.[31] In addition, he may have felt that the poem was especially deceptive in that the moralistic, orthodox, and rationalistic elements he added to it in 1786 were on the surface intended to make the earlier surrealistic, "poetic" version palatable to an audience he doubtless assumed would be generally moralistic, orthodox, and rationalistic. He may have gotten feedback that the first version, with its experimental, fancy-saturated atmosphere, was incomprehensible to its readers. Subsequently, he altered it for wider appeal, even as he privately mocked the grounds on which the appeal was made. Whatever his reasons, in 1795 Freneau slashed the 136 stanzas of the 1786 version to twenty-one consisting of the 1786 stanzas 3-17 and 119-24 and re-titled the remains "The Vision of the Night, [A Fragment]." The 1795 version omits every trace of the death-of-Death theme central to the earlier versions.

Freneau's 1786 revisions of "The Beauties of Santa Cruz" were apparently more to his liking, since he followed them almost verbatim in the 1795 and 1809 editions. Like the 1786 "House of Night," they also reflect the shift from his pre- to post-1780 definition of fancy and his corresponding shift to a relatively hard-headed rationalism. Prefacing the poem with two new quatrains which he used in 1795 in the body of the poem as stanzas 8 and 9 and which express his effort to shake off the druglike spell of the island, he equates indulgence in the nebulous romanticism of the 1779 version with moral self-deception and cowardice:

> *Sweet orange grove, the fairest of the isle,*
> *In thy soft shade luxuriously reclin'd,*
> *Where, round my fragrant bed, the flowrets smile,*
> *In sweet delusions I deceive my mind.*

> *But Melancholy's glooms assail my breast,*
> *For potent nature reigns despotic here;—*
> *A Nation ruin'd, and a world oppress'd,*
> *Might rob the boldest Stoic of a tear.*[32]

The image of the poet sprawled in flowers, daydreaming, expresses what Freneau seems by 1780 to have concluded was inherent in and wrong with fancy. It served as an escape from reality to "sweet delusions" independent of the real world. Creative it was, but its creativity served merely to "deceive" the mind. He contrasts this fantasizing about Santa Cruz's pastoral delights with the hard fact that the "nature" making the island bloom is, like oppressors everywhere, "potent" and "despotic," implying before the poem begins that the beautiful appearance of nature on Santa Cruz mirrors its reality neither on the island nor elsewhere. Central to the 1786 version is the speaker's agonized decision to face this fact by leaving the island.

The 1786 version consists of 108 stanzas, more than twice as many as in the original. Although many of the new lines merely amplify the descriptions of the island's flora and fauna presented in 1779, the most important and interesting clarify its land-sea symbolism, giving us an insight into Freneau's mature poetic technique. For example, stanzas 35-38 of the 1786 version introduce into the poem the association between land and marriage, femaleness, and domesticity made by Ralph in "The Lost Adventurer." Recounting the story of Aurelia, a "rural maid" of Santa Cruz who fell in love with the local swain Philander but who died on another island looking for him after he left her "to roam" (11. 137-52), the stanzas not only establish the link between land and sexual love and procreation, with its connotations of domestic security and female timidity, that Freneau rings countless later changes on but also give us in capsule form the plot Freneau repeatedly uses in subsequent poems, a land-based woman trying to hold on to or rejoin her seagoing man. In this formula, the sea epitomizes the restless, wandering side of the male narrator, the land his connubial, haven-seeking side.

More important, in stanza 55, also new in the 1786 version, the Freneau-narrator suddenly returns to the theme introduced in the two prefatory stanzas and identifies himself as a wanderer. "O grant me, gods, if yet condemn'd to stray," he says, "At least to spend life's sober evening here" (11. 217-18). Although he sounds unhappy about his wanderlust, in that he feels "condemn'd" by it, he does prefer it to Santa Cruz's illusoriness, figured in five new stanzas (11. 257-76) that describe the island's *Animal* flower, which closes "like a deluding dream" (1. 271) if one tries to touch it. The most important new stanza in the 1786 version, stanza 89, states this preference openly and thus defines the whole meaning of the Santa Cruz experience for the narrator and presumably Freneau himself:

> *For I must go where the mad pirate roves,*
> *A stranger on the inhospitable* main,
> *Torn from the scenes of Hudson's sweetest groves,*
> *Led by false hope, and expectation vain.*
>
> (11. 353-56)

Plainly, the narrator has chosen to abandon Santa Cruz, his island paradise, for the ocean. When he originally left "Hudson's sweetest groves," before he came to Santa Cruz for the first time, he was "Led by false hope, and expectation vain"; now, having actually visited the alleged paradise, he heads to sea, free of such illusions.

The theme of stanza 89 is reinforced by other new stanzas near it. Stanzas 83 and 84, for example, intensify the horror of the hurricane of the 1779 version by describing it from the vantage point of a ship caught at sea and by linking it to primordial forces in the universe—it is now the "Daughter of chaos, and eternal night" (1. 336). Stanzas 86 and 87 then pick up the image first struck in 1779 and repeated in the eighty-fifth stanza of the 1786 version of the hurricane's deluging the island with a figurative sea of water and expand it to show the ocean devouring the land: groves are "now with rocks and deep sands over-run" (1. 344), buildings fly "piece-meal to the seas" (1. 347). Freneau sums up the ocean's meaning in the stanzas immediately following the eighty-ninth by contrasting its lessons with the delusions that originally drew him to Santa Cruz. Stanza 90 defines the ocean:

> There *endless plains deject the wearied eye,*
> *And hostile winds incessant toil prepare;*
> *And should loud bellowing storms all art defy,*
> *The manly heart alone must conquer there.*
>
> (11. 357-60)

Although the narrator here attributes monotony, lack of aesthetic variety, unsociableness, exhausting labor, and destructiveness to the sea, he argues it is nevertheless the proving ground of the "manly heart." However unpleasant, the ocean represents the deepest realities of life itself, including death. Without a clear perception of these realities, the narrator argues, no person is mature. Moreover, the third and fourth lines of the stanza celebrate the personal courage in face of death to which Freneau was increasingly attracted in the mideighties and which he defined in his well-known letter published in *The Freeman's Journal* on July 8, 1789, as an informal stoicism. "Indeed," he wrote,

the *sea* is the *best* school for philosophy (I mean the moral kind;) in thirteen or fourteen years acquaintance with this element, I am convinced a man ought to imbibe more of your right genuine *stoical* stuff, than could be gained in half a century on shore.[33]

We also recall, of course, the complimentary reference to "the boldest Stoic" in the second of the poem's new prefatory stanzas.

In the next stanza (also new in 1786) the narrator contrasts this ocean-born stoicism with Santa Cruz by returning to the flower image of the two prefatory stanzas:

> *On these blue hills to pluck the opening flowers*
> *Might yet awhile the unwelcome task delay,*
> *And these gay scenes prolong the fleeting hours*
> *To aid bright Fancy on some future day.*
>
> (11. 361-64)

The stanza rejects the option it offers. The narrator will no longer stay in Santa Cruz indulging himself in flowery delusions. "Fancy" is by implication vicious, however "bright."

There remain to be considered two important poems published for the first time in the 1786 *Poems* without composition dates. The first, "The Vernal Ague," reveals the depth of Freneau's disenchantment by the mideighties with land and its cheerful promises. Opening with two stanzas that place the speaker on the banks of a stream in a forest grove he used to love, the poem suddenly begins repudiating these surroundings in stanza 3:

> *Yet what can please amid this bower,*
> *That charm'd my eyes for many an hour!*
> *The budding leaf is lost to me,*
> *And dead the bloom on every tree.*[34]

The stream, the songs of birds, the hills and valleys and the western breeze, the speaker goes on,

> *Have lost their charms! — the blooms are gone!*
> *Trees put a darker aspect on,*
> *The stream disgusts that wanders by,*
> *And every zephyr brings a sigh.*
>
> (11. 17-20)

He concludes the poem with a bitter prayer to "Restoring Nature" to

> *Renew these colours, that must fade,*
> *When vernal suns forbear to roll,*
> *And endless winter chills the soul.*
>
> (11. 24-26)

Like "The Hurricane," "The Vernal Ague" confronts death without benefit of softening illusion. Death is an "endless winter" that "chills the soul" to a presumably eternal iciness. There is no god to pray to save a "Restoring Nature" that may itself end in obliteration, that at best moves in cycles indifferent to the fate of individuals, and that offers only the consolation of images of natural beauty which invariably fade. Worse still, the speaker has discovered he cannot sustain his pleasure in these images, oppressed as he is by his vision of transience and death. The whole bucolic atmosphere "disgusts" him. Like "A Moral Thought," in which the withdrawal of the tide destroys the glitter of the water's surface and leaves the mud of the river-bed littered with seaweed, "The Vernal Ague" chronicles a harsh process of disillusionment.

The second poem, "Captain Jones's Invitation," once again argues that the right response to such disillusionment is stoic indifference. Aside from one brief allusion to the war with Britain in stanza 5, the poem is wholly nonpolitical in tone and subject matter, a fact Freneau acknowledged in 1795 by retitling it simply "The Invitation," thereby freeing it from distracting patriotic claims. Consisting of ten six-line stanzas in tetrameter couplets, the poem's invitation is addressed to a landsman who has seen the ocean and perhaps been attracted enough by it to sail with the speaker and discover what the sea really means. That the poem's ocean is symbolically as well as literally deep is evident in the opening stanza:

> *Thou, who on some dark mountain's brow*
> *Hast toil'd thy life away till now,*
> *And often from that rugged steep*
> *Beheld the vast extended deep,*
> *Come from thy forest, and with me*
> *Learn what it is to go to sea.*[35]

Implying that to toil one's life away in a forest is superficial and "unmanly," the speaker nevertheless hints that the lands-man who is attracted to the sea may have the moral strength necessary for a genuinely oceanic view of life. Freneau is saying that although relatively few landsmen have the fortitude to become sailors, those who do will deepen their now shallow, land-oriented lives. The "vast extended deep" seen from the mountaintop is rich with symbolic meanings from which the poem selects in succeeding stanzas one for major stress — not so much death itself but rather the common human weakness of being afraid to die. In this regard the poem seems thematically more akin to "Plato to Theon," in which, it will be recalled, the speaker chides an old man for his reluctance to die, than to any other poem of the period.

Like "The Hurricane," the "Invitation" associates the ocean primarily with death. In stanza 2 the landsman is told that out on the "endless plains" (1. 7) of the sea he will lose contact with land because the "realms of death intrude between" (1. 10). Stanza 5 warns against being led by fine weather to believe the sea is benign: "Be not deciev'd — 'tis but a show, / For many a corpse is laid below" (11. 27-28). Death through war, in which "At every blast the brave expire" (1. 33), is epitomized in stanza 6, and stanza 7 threatens shipwreck "on some leeward coast" (1. 40). But the eighth stanza is the most explicit in the poem.

> *Above us storms distract the sky,*
> *Beneath us depths unfathom'd lie,*
> *Too near we see, a ghastly sight,*
> *The realms of everlasting night,*
> *A wat'ry tomb of ocean green*
> *And only one frail plank between!*
>   (11. 43-48)

Literally, the main ocean and, symbolically, death remain "unfathom'd." The terror of the "Too near" phrase is convincing on both levels, since it suggests not merely the panic of a threatened ship but, in the striking image of "one frail plank," the shock of what has in all ages resulted from insight into the fact of one's own death. The "wat'ry tomb of ocean green," like the ocean in the poem as a whole, is more a symbol of the ocean voyager's understanding of death than of death itself. The distinction is important because what Freneau seems mainly to want to teach the landsman in the poem is the need for hard-headed, realistic self-knowledge. Such self-knowledge is impossible, he implies, if one cannot face one's own death squarely.

But the poem's argument does not end here. Beyond perception of the reality of death, it continues, lies the courage of the true seaman to accept that reality. Like the 1786 version of "Santa Cruz" and numerous other poems of this period, "The Invitation" sets forth the informal, stoic belief that human beings should meet death carelessly and without fear. Those who not only can accept the fact that they must die but can await the event calmly and without self-delusion will enjoy certain rewards, one of which is outlined in stanza 4:

> *Yet sometimes groves and meadows gay*
> *Delight the seamen on their way;*
> *From the deep seas that round us swell*
> *With rocks the surges to repel*
> *Some verdant isle, by waves embrac'd,*
> *Swells, to adorn the wat'ry waste.*
>
> (11. 19-24)

On the literal level, the image describes one's first view of an island from the deck of a ship: the island at first might appear to be a wave swelling out of the water. On the symbolic or metaphorical level, the island's swelling in this way from the water seems to be Freneau's way of saying that the person without illusions concerning death can still find and enjoy islands of moral and aesthetic refreshment in the middle of such realism. For the seaman, the main purpose of such islands is "to adorn the wat'ry waste"—that is, to soften the harsh seascape.

In the poem's penultimate stanza Freneau offers the prospective ocean voyager further consolation.

> *But winds must cease, and storms decay,*
> *Not always lasts the gloomy day,*
> *Again the skies are warm and clear,*
> *Again soft zephyrs fan the air,*
> *Again we find the long lost shore,*
> *The winds oppose our wish no more.*
>
> (11. 49-54)

Here the poem returns to a mainland similar in meaning to the coastal mountaintop of stanza 1, a mainland of harbor and refuge. Although Freneau fully explores its meaning in other poems, here he uses it simply to suggest a comfortable superficiality in contrast to the deep lessons to be learned offshore. Like the mild weather, it is a metaphor for faith that nature is benign and that humankind will enjoy immortality.

The "Invitation" ends with a ringing challenge.

> *If thou hast courage to despise*
> *The various changes of the skies,*
> *To disregard the ocean's rage,*
> *Unmov'd when hostile ships engage,*
> *Come from thy forest, and with me*
> *Learn what it is to go to sea.*
>
> (11. 55-60)

In recapitulating the forms of death he has already presented —death by drowning, death in battle—Freneau underscores the moral courage that lies at the heart of his symbolization of the ocean in the poem. The extraordinarily powerful word "despise" sums up what he means by such courage. One should not weakly resign oneself to death but instead defy it by living dangerously on the open sea. This view of the ocean as an arena of combat between human beings' will to live and the knowledge they must die saturates Freneau's ocean poetry of the eighties and absorbs all the types of human competitiveness he treats. Commerce, war, politics—risk-taking and pugnaciousness of every kind—are all predominantly linked with the sea. Thus to learn "what it is to go to sea" is to learn not only that life is in conflict with death and is itself disharmonious but that the lesson must be unflinchingly, even recklessly, lived by.

Yet the tone of "The Invitation" is unmistakably positive. Like "Plato to Theon," the poem sets out to teach naive landsmen truths that will strengthen them morally. It resembles almost every serious lyric Freneau published between 1780 and 1786 in assuming that realism is all to the good—far better, certainly, than fanciful daydreaming. When it recommends that we all should learn what it is to go to sea, the poem exudes a confidence that the lesson, however harsh, will in the long run make us better human beings. By 1788 Freneau was no longer so confident.

IV

"The Fine Delusion Ends," 1786-1788

For the next two years, through the appearance of his second collection, *The Miscellaneous Works*, in April 1788, Freneau explored the implications of the bleakly ocean-oriented view of life he had adopted. Although the poems that resulted did not openly repudiate the stoic indifference he had formulated as a response to this view of life, they nonetheless hinted at alternatives. One was a corrosive irony. There is a caustic, sardonic quality in many of the lyrics of this period that is generally not found elsewhere in his nonpolitical poetry. Another alternative was a genuinely tragic view of life, also not found in any other period of his career. A third was a resigned tolerance of humankind's capacity for self-deception. During these two years Freneau's skepticism not only carried him as close to philosophical despair as he ever came but at the same time opened the way for a new interpretation of life by subtly calling his stoicism into question.

Yet there was no sharp change in the tone or theme of his best work during these two years from that of the 1786 *Poems*. He continued to praise ocean realism and to attack the illusions of land, he often recommended stoic fortitude, and he remained depressed by his sense of universal death and transience. The first poem he published after the 1786 *Poems* was very much in the earlier mold. Currently his best-known lyric, "The Wild Honey-Suckle" appeared July 6, 1786, in the *Columbian Herald*. Essentially it restates the argument of "The Vernal Ague" in gentler terms. A honeysuckle vine in an out-of-the-way place has caught the eye of the speaker, who addresses to the vine a twenty-four-line lament concerning its transience. Although he is "Smit"[1] with the flower's beauty, he, like the speaker of "The Vernal Ague," insists that the beauty is delusive—that, as the final line asserts, the flower is nothing more than an "empty image" (1. 24). Freneau's revisions of this line in succeeding editions are significant in that they show how in the course of the following ten years the nihilism and pessimism of the *Columbian Herald* version give way to less and less harsh wording. In the *Columbian Herald* the final two lines are as follows: "The space between is but an hour,/The empty image of a flower." In the 1788 *Works* Freneau reworded this as, "The space between is but an hour,/The mere idea of a flower."[2] By 1795 the lines had been softened to, "The space between, is but an hour,/The frail duration of a flower."[3] The "empty image" of 1786 echoes Freneau's post-1780 attack not only on fancy, with its fabrication of hollow and delusive poetic fables, but on all kinds of land-inspired illusion. By 1795, having gone through a revolution in his thought against this sea-oriented skepticism, Freneau settled on the far more sympathetic phrase "frail duration." Similar softenings are apparent at two other points in the poem. In 1786 the flower's setting is called a "dreary dark retreat" (1. 2); in 1795 it has become the somewhat less depressing "silent, dull retreat." In 1786 the speaker bluntly defines the flower's existence as a "life declining to repose" (1. 12), but in 1795 he euphemizes it to "days declining to repose."

In the original 1786 version, then, the speaker's dissatisfaction with this beautiful but deceptive land-based natural object is clear. The pastoral setting, like that of "The Vernal Ague," is disappointing; not only is it "dreary" and "dark" but, more important, it leads the speaker to the kind of depression voiced in the earlier poem. The final stanza argues that life—or at least a flower's life—is simply a phase in the meaningless and indifferent cycles of nature.[4] Life and death are indistinguishable.

> From morning suns and evening dews
> At first thy little being came—
> If nothing once—you nothing lose,
> For when you die you are the same—
> The space between is but an hour,
> The empty image of a flower.
>
> (11. 19-24)

The question implied throughout the poem, of course, is whether the speaker and, beyond him, all humankind share a similar fate. By giving the flower human characteristics in the first two stanzas—its branches "meet" (1. 4) each other, it produces a "tear" (1. 6) when its stem is broken, it is "array'd" (1. 7) in white and shuns the "vulgar eye" (1. 8) like a shy maiden—the speaker suggests two contradictory ways of answering the question. The first is that the personification is purely figurative and is designed to underline the fact that the speaker is not a flower and the flower is not a human being. The concluding stanzas seem to bear this out by insisting on the flower's spiritual and intellectual emptiness, which stands in sharp contrast to the speaker's percipience. On the other hand, the personification can be interpreted as suggesting direct parallels between human and plant experience, an interpretation buttressed by the striking allusion in stanza 3 to Eden:

> *(They died—nor were those flowers less gay,*
> *The flowers that did in Eden bloom). . . .*
> (11.15-16)

The insinuation is that, like human beings, flowers fell from grace and became mortal.

The poem does not answer the question definitively, revealing once again Freneau's lifelong tentativeness regarding the possibility of life after death. Concerning the flowers, though, it is explicit. The flower has no existence beyond blind natural process except as an image in the poet's mind. The poem insists on a realistic understanding of nature far removed from the romantic vision of *The American Village* poems. Wild honeysuckles have no thoughts or feelings, regardless of poetic efforts to personify them. They are as delusive as the beauties of "Santa Cruz" or the landscape of "The Vernal Ague." The kind of conversation or communion between a flower and a human being attempted in the poem is impossible, because flower and human being inhabit utterly different spheres of existence. Only in the symbolic sense of possibly sharing a nihilistic destiny can flower and human being be said to be the same, and, as indicated earlier, this is merely one of the interpretations the poem can sustain.

Equally stern and uncompromising is a poem that appeared nine months later in *The Freeman's Journal*. Titled "The Departure," the poem is Freneau's fullest and most elegant statement of the somber ideas he had been developing and putting forth piecemeal in serious verse since 1780. Grave and stately, it consists of eighty-five irregular lines that express the speaker's thoughts as he watches the coastline at the mouth of the Hudson River drop astern his ocean-bound ship in a cold, late-autumn sunset. The opening stanza introduces the theme of the futility of pursuing happiness which dominates the poem.

> *From Hudson's cold, congealing streams*
> *As winter comes, I take my way*

Where other suns prompt other dreams,
And shades less willing to decay
Beget new raptures in the heart,
Bid spleen's dejective crew depart,
And wake the sprightly lay.[5]

Although the speaker knows he will find "other suns" in the tropical latitudes ahead, he also knows they are no less transient than the summer suns of New York, now gone, and will simply provoke "other dreams"—the word "dreams" here connoting, as usual in the poems of the eighties, fantasy, escape from truth, self-delusion. And though the "shades," or tree leaves, to the south are "less willing to decay" than those of the land behind him, decay they must, so that the "raptures" and cheerful songs they inspire will be in a universal sense as unrealistic and unjustifiable as if they had been written in the leafless forests of New Jersey.

Next the speaker turns from the land to contemplate the ocean around and beneath him.

Good-natur'd Neptune, now so mild—
Like rage asleep, or madness chain'd—
By dreams amus'd, or love beguil'd,
Sleep on—'till we our port have gain'd.
The gentle breeze, that curls the deep,
Shall paint a finer dream on sleep!—
Ye nymphs, that haunt his grottoes low,
Where sea-green trees on coral grow—
   No tumults make,
   Lest he should wake;
And, thus, the passing shade betray
The sails that o'er his waters stray.

(11. 8-19)

Personification of the sea as a potential demon of rage and destruction needs no explanation in the context of poems like

"The Hurricane" and "Port Royal." The speaker's petition to this now literally unconscious and unhearing god of the sea is ironic. Your kindest favor, Neptune, says Freneau, will be to ignore me altogether since to gain your attention means, in effect, to die.

The relatively cheerful tone of the first two stanzas gives way in the third to a majesty gravity of thought and style.

> *Sunk is the sun from yonder hill;*
> *The noisy day is past;*
> *The breeze decays, and all is still,*
> *As all shall be at last;*
> *The murmuring on the distant shore,*
> *The dying wave is all I hear;*
> *The yellow fields now disappear,*
> *No painted butterflies are near,*
> *And laughing folly plagues no more.*
>
> (11. 20-28)

The entire experience—the oncoming darkness and stillness, the coast blurring in the distance—is a powerful image of departure at several levels: from land to sea, shallowness to depth, life to death. The speaker neither dies nor intends to die, of course, yet the ocean scene around him hints of how still it will be when "all shall be at last." The final line drives home the stanza's symbolic meaning. "Laughing folly," allegedly as characteristic of land as "painted butterflies," is by implication not found at sea, which of course is true only in the framework of Freneau's land-sea symbolism. Linked as they are with "laughing folly," the "painted butterflies" suggest superficial landsmen who lack the spiritual maturity of the person who has ventured oceanward. The speaker's disgust with land here is as harsh as in "The Vernal Ague."

The next two stanzas introduce the seasonal death of plant life on shore as a corollary image, like the transient landscape of "The Vernal Ague" and the ephemeral honeysuckle, of the inevitable dissolution of all things in physical nature. Then Freneau returns to the ocean in stanza 6 and, as in "The Invitation," defies it.

> *Now, while I spread the vent'rous sail*
> *To catch the breeze from yonder hill,*
> *Say, what does all this folly mean —?*
> *Why grieve to pass the wat'ry scene —?*
> *Is happiness to* place *confin'd —?*
> *No — planted only in the mind,*
> *She makes an* Eden *where she will.*
>
> (11.53-59)

Freneau substantially revised the final three lines of this stanza for the 1788 *Works*, where they read,

> *Is fortitude to heaven confin'd —?*
> *No — planted also in the mind,*
> *She smooths the ocean when she will.*[6]

The original lines offer more hope for achieving happiness than do the rewritten lines composed less than a year later. Sensing that they contradicted the deeply pessimistic drift of the poem as a whole, suggesting as they do, probably inadvertently, that one can be happy no matter where one is, he brought them into line with the stoicism of his major sea poems of the preceding three years. It seems clear that the "Eden" referred to in the earlier version was in any case meant ironically: Freneau's consistent argument throughout the mideighties and in the rest of "The Departure" that happiness is a delusion forces us to see in the remark the bitter and sarcastic suggestion that humankind's tendency to create fanciful Edens is self-deluding. In the original version, the lines suggest a more sympathetic reading, which Freneau must have wished to forestall. In the revised version, Freneau's grief at having to cross the ocean reflects his abhorrence not only of his own death

but of a universe in which all things must die. But he chides
himself at the "folly" of such a lament and in an explicitly
symbolic phrase "smooths the ocean" through sheer moral
courage. He will conquer his repugnance to death by an act of
will. The metaphor of spreading the "vent'rous" sail suggests,
as in many other poems, his determination to treat death as
the final challenge, the last great adventure, even though he
suspects it may reveal nothingness.

Stanza 7 opens with the abrupt statement "But man must
groan" (1. 60) ("But life is pain" in the 1788 *Works*). The
poem then goes on in the rest of stanza 7 and the first half of
stanza 8 to list some of life's evils: malice, calumny, indifference, slander, ignorance, cowardice, pride, disgust, and servility.
Paraphrased, the passage argues that one needs as much fortitude to face life—to return to land and its human viciousness
—as to face the ocean of death, a fact that leads the speaker
to long wistfully for the original golden paradise in which nature did not decay and the evils he has just described did not
"disgrace the mind" or "haunt the human breast" (11. 71-72).
Yet he asserts that this paradise is "vanish'd" (1. 74), and in
the final stanza of the poem he doubts it can be recovered in
another state of being.

> *What season shall restore that scene*
> *When all was calm, and all serene,*
> *And* Happiness *no empty sound,*
> *The golden age that pleas'd so well—?*
> *The mind that made it shall not tell*
> *To those on life's uncertain road;*
> *Where, lost in folly's idle round,*
> *And seeking what shall ne'er be found,*
> *We press to one abode.*
>
> (11. 77-85)

Freneau's use of the idea of a golden age in the past, a period of primitive simplicity and innocence, is here a literary device against which he can hold up the real world of the present for rhetorical effect. Even if such an age did once exist, as classical pagans and orthodox Christians claim, its reappearance depends, Freneau argues, on a supernal "mind" that no longer communicates with human beings. The three final lines recapitulate Freneau's argument throughout the poem: the living, all of whom pursue spurious fantasies of mortal or immortal happiness, are relentlessly pursued by death, the only absolute certainty of their lives.

Freneau's poem, then, signifies a departure from far more than New York harbor. It sums up his departure from delusion concerning life to realism concerning death; from orthodox habits of mind to unorthodox speculation; from conventional eighteenth-century poetic techniques to a symbolic mode unique in the poetry of the age. It gathers the threads of his deepest thought and feeling during the 1780s and weaves them together with superlative subtlety, precision, and force. It is perhaps his finest achievement and surely one of the great poems in American literature.

Poems similar in tone and statement to "The Wild Honey-Suckle" and "The Departure" were "May to April," published April 18, 1787, in *The Freeman's Journal*, and "Address to Misfortune," printed three months later in the same newspaper. Far different, though, were "The Roguish Shoemaker: In Imitation of Watts's Indian Philosopher" and "St. Preux to Eloisa," which were covert attacks against Christianity and Rousseauian sentimentality, respectively. These two poems are suffused with the irony that is often found in Freneau's writing between 1786 and 1788 and that tends to belie its praise of stoic indifference. Freneau was simply not the kind of man who could remain resigned or indifferent to what he perceived as wrongheadedness no matter how *dégagé* he tried or wanted to be, and in "The Roguish Shoemaker" he mounts

a stinging attack against Christian orthodoxy. He became acquainted with the works of Isaac Watts, tireless defender of
protestant Christianity and enemy of Restoration wit and
libertinism, at least as early as 1769, when he glossed a section
of the fifth volume of Watts's *Works* and signed the gloss "1769
Princeton College."[7] Virtually all of Freneau's other marginalia
in the book are hostile: at one point, for instance, he says of
Watts's argument, "It is easy to set up a Man of Straw and then
knock him down" (p. 358); at another, jeeringly, "Ha! ha! ha!"
(p. 386); and at still another, "The Doctor or Printer are in an
Error here: Some parts of America are not more than a 1000
Leagues from Europe" (p. 481).

Part of Freneau's reason for choosing Watts as his target in
"The Roguish Shoemaker" was doubtless Watts's extraordinary
popularity in America in the second half of the eighteenth
century. At least six editions of Watts's *Horae Lyricae: Poems
chiefly of The Lyric Kind*, which first appeared in England in
1709, were printed in America between 1760 and 1800. Since
Watts was the best-known anti-Enlightenment Christian apolo-
gist of the day in America, Freneau hoped that by burlesquing
him he would make his point clear to kindred freethinkers
even if out of prudence he chose, as he did, to parody one of
Watts's more secular efforts. Watts's "The Indian Philosopher,"
addressed to Henry Bendish and dated September 3, 1701, is
a fanciful explanation of the cause of marital friction. The
speaker recounts a dream in which he hears an Indian holy
man on the banks of the Ganges expound the Eastern doctrine
that souls are paired before birth and sent together to earth to
find bodies. Unfortunately, most of these pairs are separated
on the way, many ending up in Europe and their mates in
Asia. The most obvious key to Freneau's satire is his punning
on Watts's use of the word "soul." In his fifth stanza, for example, Watts's holy man speaks of

'. . . th' Eternal rolling Flame,
'That vital Mass, that still the same
   'Does all our minds compose:
'But shap'd in twice ten thousand Frames;
'Thence diff'ring Souls of diff'ring Names,
   'And jarring Tempers rose.[8]

Freneau's shoemaker paraphrases the stanza thus:

. . . "The spacious ample hide
"That does for all our hoofs provide,
   "Should still be free from blame,
"For shap'd into so many soals,
"Some would have flaws, and some have holes,
   "Just as by chance it came.[9]

Freneau insinuates throughout that Christian priests resemble his unctuous, long-winded, self-rationalizing, and ultimately dishonest cobbler, who is the line-for-line, stanza-for-stanza counterpart of Watts's Indian holy man. Particularly insulting are Freneau's continual hints that priests, like shoemakers, manufacture fables, just as Watts's Indian does. The cobbler's fable—that is, his answer to the speaker's query about why shoes wear out so quickly—seems to be a covert attack by Freneau on the Christian doctrine of original sin. Having argued in the stanza just quoted that the great Ur-hide—a parody of Watts's "Eternal Rolling Flame," or creative principle of nature—is not to blame for bad shoes, the shoemaker goes on to assert that the great Ur-shoemaker—Watts's "mighty Power that form'd the Mind" (1. 31), or universal principle of intelligence—is also blameless. The real problem, he says, is that

". . . when these hides had left the vat,
"Lodg'd in our shop, a hungry rat
   "Attacks them with his jaws—

"Ah! cruel chance, and ragged fate!
"He gnaw'd them early, gnaw'd them late,
  "For hunger has no laws.
                (11. 37-42)

By "rat" Freneau seems to mean Satan, who according to the
doctrine of original sin vitiates the soul before birth. That Freneau had in mind the soul and its preterrestrial experience in
these lines is strongly suggested by the corresponding lines in
Watts's poem:

"But parting from their warm Abode
"They lost their Fellows on the Road,
  "And never join'd their Hands:
"Ah cruel Chance, and crossing Fates!
"Our Eastern *Souls have dropt their Mates*
  "On Europe's *barbarous Lands.*
                (11. 37-42)

Watts's "warm Abode" is of course heaven, which Freneau
amusingly changed to the "vat" from which mortal souls (soles)
emanate.

The pains Freneau took to screen his irreverent satire from
common view are evident not only in the fact that he chose
to parody one of Watts's more secular poems but also in the
fact that his own poem is made to seem highly topical: it pre-
tends to recount a real speech by a real cobbler concerning a
real crisis in Charleston shoemaking. Yet the poem contains
so many hints of wider meaning tied to Watts's that it makes a
purely literal reading impossible. Moreover, although Watts did
not introduce specifically Christian elements into the poem,
he did describe all the poems in this section of the *Horae Lyricae* as 'sacred to Virtue, Honour, and Friendship" and did
preface "The Indian Philosopher" with a prose note to Bendish
that sets forth an argument startlingly similar to that of Freneau's "Advertisement" to the 1786 "House of Night".

I persuade myself you will accept from the Press what the Pen more privately inscrib'd to you long ago; and I'm in no Pain lest you should take Offence at the fabulous Dress of this Poem: Nor would weaker Minds be scandaliz'd at it, if they would give themselves leave to reflect how many divine Truths are spoken by the Holy Writers in Vision and Images, Parables and Dreams: Nor are my wiser Friends asham'd to defend it, since the narrative is grave and the Moral so just and obvious. (p. 146)

We can imagine Freneau's malicious smile at this. Christians of the Watts variety would most certainly be "scandaliz'd" at his parody, were they to see its real meaning; his parable ridicules the "Holy Writers" and the whole establishment, especially priests like Watts, which their Bible created. Watts tries seriously to justify the "fabulous Dress" of his poem by stressing its unexceptionable morality; not many months before, Freneau had used the same argument, ironically, to launch the "House of Night."

On the other hand, "St. Preux to Eloisa" is a mordant, twenty-five line satire on the sentimental doctrines of Rousseau's notorious 1761 *Julie, ou La Nouvelle Héloïse*. Probably the most widely read and influential sentimental novel of its time, *La Nouvelle Héloïse* chronicles the love affair of Julie Étange, daughter of an inflexibly class-prejudiced, Swiss nobleman, and St. Preux, her common-born tutor. Freneau's poem was apparently only indirectly inspired by Rousseau's novel. What seems to have triggered it was a poem by Henry Mackenzie entitled "The Sentimental Sailor; or St. Preux to Eloisa." That Freneau had Mackenzie's poem in mind when he wrote his own is evidenced not only by the title but by the fact that Freneau's bookseller friend Robert Bell, whom Freneau had elegized in *The Freeman's Journal* six weeks before "St. Preux to Eloisa" appeared, had in 1782 printed the first American edition of Mackenzie's *The Man of Feeling* with "The Sentimental Sailor" as an afterpiece. In the poem, Mackenzie expands St. Preux's four-page account of his voyage into an eighteen-page torrent of St. Preux's passion for Julie, complete with his own agitated explanatory notes. The tone of the poem can be inferred from the three-page, prose "Introduction" with which Mackenzie prefaced it. "The story of the nightingale," he says at one point, "singing with her breast against a thorn, may, with sufficient propriety, be applied to the muses. Poetry is never so flowing and harmonious, so universally pleasing and affecting, as when, inspired by deep distress, she utters, in genuine language of nature, the voice of unavailing woe."[10]

Freneau ridicules both Rousseau and Mackenzie by giving St. Preux the footloose, somewhat rakish character of the ad-venturer-sailor we have already met in poems like "The Lost Adventurer" and the 1786 "Santa Cruz." Unlike anything St. Preux says in Rousseau's novel or Mackenzie's poem, Freneau has him begin by claiming he

> . . . a secret pleasure had
> In rambling to and fro',
> Which they that always stay at home,
> Like lazy plants, untaught to roam—
> Which they shall never know.[11]

This is absolute heresy to the spirit of the novel and the poem. In them, St. Preux is a vegetable when he is separated from Julie. Freneau continues the joke by insinuating that the reason St. Preux left France was that a group of sailors had lured him away with seedy promises, hinted at in the third stanza of Freneau's poem. In the stanza, St. Preux makes the ludicrously un-Rousseauian comment that it will be too bad if his ship goes aground on some oriental island because then, rather than getting back to enjoy Eloisa's "arms" (1. 17), he will have to content himself with "some swarthy dame" (1. 18) of the south seas.

But it is in the final stanza that Freneau gets to the heart of his attack. Says St. Preux,

Yet love, with undiminish'd joy,
Shall trace your form in fancy's glass,
While I more fond, and you, less coy,
O'er swelling seas together pass—
No rocks nor seas can love divide,
Where heart with heart is thus ally'd.

(11. 20-25)

St. Preux will have these consoling thoughts when he is living with his swarthy inamorata, thoughts that mercilessly probe the major weakness in Rousseau's novel—Julie's and St. Preux's unwillingness to elope. Rousseau covers this bald spot by making Julie so tenderhearted that she cannot bear to upset her tyrannical father by running away with St. Preux. Freneau satirically implies that the real reason for their not solving the problem by eloping is that St. Preux on the one hand did not love Julie enough to demand it and Julie on the other was too much of a coquette to comply. Reflecting on the situation from the fleshpots of his island, St. Preux will chide himself for not being "more fond" and her for not being "less coy." The poem's last two lines sum up Freneau's argument: if two lovers were really as mad about each other as Rousseau claims these two were, they would never have let themselves be separated by oceans and continents but would have crossed them together at any cost. By having St. Preux admit this point, one the novel of course never does, Freneau turns Rousseau's argument upside down. What St. Preux really learned or should have learned at sea, Freneau implies, is that he and Eloisa, along with Rousseau himself, are sentimental frauds. In this one brief poem Freneau attacks romantic sentimentalism and argues for his own ocean-oriented realism, dealing Rousseau and Mackenzie telling blows along the way. It is a satiric tour de force.

Currents of irony also flow through two of the best-known poems Freneau published in 1787, both about American Indians: "The Indian Student, or Force of Nature" and "Lines

Occasioned by a visit to an old Indian burying ground," the latter just in time to be included in the 1788 *Works*. In approaching these pieces, it should be borne in mind that Freneau's interest in Indians seems to have been minimal. Although he wrote a half-dozen poems about them and a series of essays using the Indian chief Tomo-Cheeki as his persona, there is no evidence that the Indian Question was ever much on his mind. As we have seen, "The Dying Indian" is merely a ruse behind which Freneau questions the Christian mythology of death, and the Colma-Caffraro episode in "The American Village" is plainly propagandistic, as are "The Prophecy of King Tammany," published in 1782, and virtually the entire Tomo-Cheeki series. There is in fact some evidence that Freneau shared the antipathy toward Indians felt by most white Americans of his age.[12] He seems to have found the Indian most useful as a propagandistic device—as, that is, the pastoral nobleman of nature indigenous to the New World whom European decadence had destroyed. By implication, the Indian also imaged the white American swain who had to defend himself against that same decadence or likewise face destruction.

"The Indian Student," although not so blatantly propagandistic as "The Prophecy of King Tammany," was unquestionably motivated by political considerations akin to those just mentioned. In this case, however, Freneau attacks not only the general unnaturalness of white, European civilization but, specifically, the self-complacence and bigotry of New England Calvinism. By 1787 he had accumulated many literary as well as philosophical grudges against the intelligentsia of New England, and in "The Indian Student" he gives some of them voice. Interpreting the poem is complicated by the fact that Freneau drastically revised it between June 20, 1787, when it appeared in *The Freeman's Journal*, and the following year when it appeared in the *Miscellaneous Works*; however, in both versions the hero, an Iroquois lad again named Shalum in the *Freeman's*

Journal version, goes from his forest home specifically to Harvard College to study, tires of the white man's book learning, and escapes back to the forest. A significant change between the first and second versions is that in the first Shalum's tribe sends him to Harvard, whereas in the second he is recruited by New Englanders. Accordingly, more onus is placed on New England in the second than in the first version, suggesting Freneau's own sense of the poem's meaning. Highly sentimental-sounding, both versions conflict in this respect with the realistic, pessimistic thrust of Freneau's thought at the time. Especially inconsistent are hints that Shalum will find true happiness back in nature. Longing while he is at Cambridge for "the shady bank, the purling stream" and "The woody wild,"[13] he finally heeds the call of the wild—the "Force of Nature" of the subtitle—and returns, to his own and his tribe's joy, "to the rural reign" (1. 45).

"Lines Occasioned by a visit to an old Indian burying ground," published five months later in November 1787, also has ironic overtones. Its opening stanzas raise issues strikingly similar to those of "The Dying Indian" four years earlier:

> *In spite of all the learn'd have said,*
> *I still my old opinion keep;*
> *The posture that we give the dead*
> *Points out the soul's eternal sleep.*

> *Not so the ancients of these lands—*
> *The Indian, when from life releas'd,*
> *Again is seated with his friends,*
> *And shares again the joyous feast.*[14]

Unlike his approach in "The Dying Indian," however, Freneau here openly links the central death mythology of his own culture with that of the Indians. In arguing that Christians bury their dead as though they believe they will never rise, he not only insinuates that civilized human beings thus tacitly grant the possibility that the soul is not immortal but also that the rationalism which underlies the civilizing process inevitably calls into question the childish optimism of primitive burial procedures like those of the Indians. The poem's cheerful lilt often masks sardonic undertones, as when the speaker blandly says,

> *His bow for action ready bent,*
> *And arrows, with a head of bone,*
> *Can only mean that life is spent,*
> *And not the finer essence gone. . . .*
> (11. 13-16)

For nearly a decade Freneau had been challenging such soothing fables of death and acknowledging the possibility of far grimmer alternatives. In asserting that the Indian style of burial "can only mean" the soul is immortal, he verges on sarcasm. Propping a carcass in a sitting position hardly proves it will live forever, no matter how many bows and arrows one puts around it. The theme of fraud is repeated and joked on a stanza later when the speaker tells future visitors to the gravesite, "No fraud upon the dead commit" (1. 18). The Indian bodies are not supine, as a reasonable person might expect: "They do not lie, but here they sit" (1. 20). Freneau's pun on the word "lie" implies the reverse of what he seems to say. In hoping to overcome death in this easy manner, the Indians most assuredly do lie, at least to themselves, the absurdity of their sitting position being underscored by the childishness of the line's diction. The "fraud" being committed is the Indian's self-delusion about immortality, though of course it applies to any civilized people as well who fail to question their own immortality.

The signal-word "fancy" occurs in stanza 6:

> *Here, still a lofty rock remains,*
> *On which the curious eye may trace*

> *(Now wasted half by wearing rains)*
> *The fancies of a ruder race.*
>
> (11. 21-24)

The Indians' "fancies" include the burial ritual as well as the artifacts on the rock. Throughout the eighties, as we have seen, Freneau voices a general distrust in the purely creative or poetic faculty of mind, implying that it encourages flight from empirical reality and reason into self-delusion. The tangle of belief and ritual that produced Indian art also produced Indian burial practices, and insofar as both are purely fanciful they are untrustworthy. Natural processes, like the rain eroding the rock, prove their mutability.

The concluding four stanzas form a unit that deserves full quotation.

> *Here, still an aged elm aspires;*
> *Beneath whose far projecting shade,*
> *(And which the shepherd still admires)*
> *The children of the forest play'd.*
>
> *There, oft' a restless Indian queen,*
> *(Pale Marian, with her braided hair)*
> *And many a barb'rous form is seen*
> *To chide the man that lingers there.*
>
> *By midnight moons, o'er moist'ning dews,*
> *In vestments for the chace array'd,*
> *The hunter still the deer pursues,*
> *The hunter, and the deer—a shade.*
>
> *And long shall tim'rous fancy see*
> *The painted chief, and pointed spear,*
> *And reason's self shall bow the knee*
> *To shadows and delusions here.*
>
> (11. 25-40)

All the action of these stanzas clusters symbolically under the "far projecting shade" of the "aged elm." Like "The Dying Elm," this elm also represents poetic dreams, though here its classical associations with death are even more explicit. It is "aged" in the sense that humankind's fanciful impulses are as old as humankind itself, and its "shade" is "far projecting" in the sense that the same impulse will continue to exist as long as humankind exists. The parenthetical comment that "the shepherd still admires" the elm seems to be Freneau's way of saying that the poet of nature—the "shepherd" he himself was in the seventies—continues to find pleasure and consolation in imagining an Arcadian relationship between humankind and the natural world.

It is within the circle of romantic fancy defined by the elm that the shepherd-poet-speaker envisions the Indian ghosts of the next two stanzas: the Indian queen, the barbarous forms, the hunter pursuing the deer. Returning in the final stanza to the idea that the impulse to fancify in this fashion is inherent in human beings, the speaker apologizes for it in several ways. It is "tim'rous," and deservedly so, because what it produces are merely "shadows and delusions." Although within the enchanted circle of the elm "reason's self" may be obliged to pay homage to fancy, it does so only in the sense that humankind's capacity for self-delusion is so great that reason will never fully control it. Far from celebrating the fanciful superstitiousness that led the Indians to put their cadavers in a sitting position, the poem argues that it is at best harmless. Far superior is reason, whose preferability is implied throughout the poem and explicitly granted in the next-to-last line. There, "reason's self" plainly carries the connotation of almost worshipful respect, as if the speaker is saying even reason itself, the arbiter, should grant at least the seductiveness, if not the truth, of fancy's delusions.[15]

Yet "The Indian Burying Ground" in tone as well as argument does seem to grant that such superstitions, however silly and childish, are both at best and at worst harmless. Contrary to the bitter attack against land-spawned illusions in poems like "The Departure" and the 1786 "Santa Cruz," "The Indian Burying Ground" seems to accept this human weakness as an unavoidable fact and to grant its influence on human affairs. Although it no more approves fancy than any of the poems Freneau had published since 1780, the poem marks a shift on Freneau's part from open hostility toward fancy to ironic acceptance of it. Its tone is in this sense consistent with that of a revealing poem Freneau published in the Charleston *City Gazette* January 30, 1788, too late to be included in the *Miscellaneous Works*. Left untitled in the *City Gazette* but called "To Lydia" in the 1795 and 1809 editions, it is the only seduction poem Freneau published. Adding to its interest is the fact that in 1795 Freneau more than doubled its length, from eleven to twenty-five stanzas, and in 1809 attached to a verbatim reprint of the 1795 version the anachronistic note that the poem was addressed to "Miss Lydia Morris, a young quaker lady, on her landing from the sloop Industry, at Savannah, in Georgia, December 30th 1806."[16] This is the kind of dating legerdemain that undercuts the reliability of Freneau's dating of most of his poems. The 1795 revision does not significantly change the poem's meaning but heightens its sexual nuances on the one hand and dampens its symbolic nuances on the other. In both versions, the poem consists of a witty, gather-ye-rosebuds-while-ye-may plea by a poetical ship captain to a beautiful female passenger to remain on his ship and become his mistress.

The original version falls into two parts, a seven-stanza recapitulation of the voyage they have just completed and a four-stanza proposition to the young woman to remain on board.

The key event of the voyage was a storm which presumably frightened the young woman into asking, for the first time in her life, questions remarkably like those Freneau had been asking of nature since 1780. In stanza 4 she deplores the storm, during which "foaming seas to mountains grow/On gulphs of death conceal'd below"[17] —lines that link this ocean to the symbolic ocean of "The Hurricane," "The Departure," and other poems we have seen in this discussion. In stanza 5 she seeks further reassurance, bidding him tell her "true/What lands again would rise to view" (11. 19-20). The speaker in stanza 6 reports the young woman's final paroxysm of doubt.

> *When night came on with blust'ring gale,*
> *You fear'd the tempest would prevail,*
> *And anxious ask'd, if I was sure*
> *That on this globe we sail'd secure?*
>
> (11. 21-24)

The question is patently broader in scope than the literal situation demands. It suggests that this innocent young creature of the land has come to doubt, either because of an actual storm or because of philosophical conversation with the sea-wise captain, whether the very earth is "secure." She in effect expresses the fear which Freneau himself expressed in "The Hurricane" that chaos may lie at the heart of nature and that the apparent solidity and permanence of the "globe" may be a delusion. Like the hurricane of the earlier poem, this "tempest" may also "prevail."

At this crucial point the speaker dismisses the young woman's point of view and gives his own reaction to the situation, which is that her beauty is a consolation against the storm:

> *Delighted with a face so fair*
> *I half forgot my weight of care,*
> *And saw, unmov'd, the whirlwind rise,*
> *Encircled moons, and threatening skies.*
>
> (11. 25-28)

Although he only half forgets his "care," a word Freneau uses throughout his sea poetry to denote intellectual as well as commercial or physical hardship, he is able to contemplate even nature's "whirlwind"—an image strikingly similar to the Lucretian vortex of whirling atoms—calmly. The beauty of this young woman's face, a synecdoche for the spiritual and sexual love she embodies, at least momentarily soothes him, allaying his suspicion that existence may be meaningless.

The poem then shifts to the present time, of their having reached shore, and to the captain's proposition she stay on board as his mistress. What is intriguing here is that, despite his obvious attraction to the young woman, the ship captain-speaker is unwilling to give up the sea for her. The notion of having an affair on a ship is so obviously whimsical and figurative as to make reading the poem as literal autobiography impossible. It may, of course, be autobiographical in a more indirect way. If addressed to a woman on land like Eleanor Forman, it might have been intended as an invitation to an extramarital sexual adventure. But a more persuasive reading, I think, is to see the voyage and the seduction as a device that allows Freneau to explore the reality-delusion theme in the fresh manner already suggested. In this context, the proposition amounts, first, to the speaker's asking an unmistakably land-oriented person to venture with him out on the seas of philosophical speculation and, second, to his grudging admission that the land, especially as embodied in a beautiful young woman, offers attractive diversion from the rigors of such sternly masculine thought. The young woman in this sense represents the type of necessary illusion produced by the elm of "The Indian Burying Ground." Two lines in the ninth stanza strongly support the idea that the relationship between the captain and the woman is ideational. Says he, "To all your questions—*when* or *why*—?/I still will make a kind reply" (11. 33-34). The questions "*when* or *why*," having no frame of reference other than the ones she asks about the earth's security, suggest ontological and eschatological problems of precisely the kind Freneau had been wrestling with for years. In saying he will answer them kindly, the captain implies that in his effort to keep her with him on his alarming speculative voyages he has only hinted to her the bleak possibilities buried in poems like "The Hurricane" and "The Departure."

Thus, despite recommendations in poems like "The Departure" to go to sea and leave the follies of land firmly astern, Freneau could not resist poetic glances shoreward. Although all these glances were ironic and derogatory, several, like "The Indian Burying Ground" and "To Lydia," signaled a willingness to tolerate human self-deception as a necessary evil. But they were premature signals. In late April 1788, *The Miscellaneous Works of Mr. Philip Freneau* appeared. Unlike the 1786 *Poems*, this collection was organized thematically rather than chronologically, with the result that it is far more intellectually coherent than its predecessor. Unifying it is the familiar land-sea dichotomy, set forth and ruminated on chiefly in the volume's poetry, and a tone of pessimism concerning both nature and humankind that, however occasionally sugared with humor and good spirits, sets it apart as the most somber book Freneau ever produced.

The collection's relative tightness of plan is clear from the start. It opens with two long narrative poems, "The Pictures of Columbus, the Genoese," and "The Hermit of Saba," which between them define the poles of the land-sea dichotomy as Freneau had come to understand it by 1788 and which are unmistakably tragic in tone. On the one hand, "The Pictures of Columbus" portrays Freneau's archetypal ocean voyager, Columbus, as the unwitting yet tragically culpable corrupter of pastoral innocence in the New World; on the other, "The Hermit of Saba" portrays an archetypal hermit figure who has deliberately withdrawn from civilization in order to escape its contaminations—he is in this respect the exact obverse of the Columbuslike explorer—yet suffers tragic defeat. Introducing the collection, "Columbus" and "Saba" establish a frame of reference within which everything else in the collection develops.

Although Freneau characteristically confused the situation by claiming in the 1795 edition that "Columbus" was written "Anno 1774,"[18] thereby encouraging the inference that the poem does not reflect his mature thought, in doing so he was probably trying to outmaneuver Joel Barlow, whose "Vision of Columbus" had appeared in 1787, by suggesting that his poem, though published after Barlow's, had actually been written more than a decade earlier. Freneau's title suggests cognizance and perhaps mockery of Barlow's poem. Freneau seems to be pointing a ridiculing finger at Barlow's awkward and meretricious device of basing a poem on a miraculous vision Columbus experiences in jail at the end of his life: his own "Pictures" of Columbus, he implies, will explore the meaning of Columbus's career more honestly, intelligently, and realistically. As is well known, Barlow's central thesis is that the key to post-Columbian American greatness lay in successful international commerce. By contrast, Freneau had come by the late eighties to see such commerce, especially as it was practiced by aristocratic, Anglophiliac New Englanders, as a major threat to America's well-being. Hence in "The Pictures of Columbus" he condemns Columbus's expedient appeal to the avarice of both his patrons and his crew by having him not only suffer personal disgrace but emerge as the single individual most responsible for infecting the New World with decadent European commerce, figured in the poem by Columbus's condoning of the enslavement of the Indians and the plundering of their gold. Thus although it is possible that Freneau drafted a version of "The Pictures of Columbus" during the seventies, it seems virtually certain that, like many others he gave an early date, the poem is substantially the product of the period in which it was first issued.

The major intellectual issue raised in the poem is the familiar fancy-reason debate. In "Picture I" Columbus, not satisfied with his "Gay, painted picture of the mind"[19] of land to the west, asserts, "O'er real seas I mean to sail" (p. 2) in order to verify it. Driving him on is the personal ambition revealed in his remark that "Worlds yet unthought of shall be mine" (p. 2). He wants to ascertain whether the land his "Fancy" (p. 2) has created exists in fact; and thus we are thrust immediately into the fancy-reason, delusion-reality dichotomies that pervade Freneau's mideighties verse. This initial "Picture," Columbus's imaginative leap to the New World, provokes the remaining "Pictures" of the poem, thereby establishing imaginative boldness not only as the cause of the subsequent corruption of New-World innocence but, more positively, as the parent of civilized America. Columbus's intellectual venturesomeness is accordingly both bad and good. It simultaneously destroys innocence and advances humankind's material and intellectual horizons. As we have seen, this ambivalence toward ocean voyaging is apparent in all of Freneau's most searching poems of the sea. To venture out on uncharted seas of thought is preferable to the comfortable complacency of land, yet what one either discovers or causes to happen as a result can be appalling. Without the restless wanderlust of a Columbus, America would have remained unknown to Europeans. Paradoxically, it would thus have been spared European depravity. Columbus the wanderer is Ralph of "The Lost Adventurer" writ large.[20]

The eighteenth and final "Picture" of the poem, "Columbus at Valladolid," sets forth Freneau's invariable post-1780 assessment: reason is realistic and superior to fancy, which is delusive. Only if fancy is empirically verifiable and consistent with reason is it valuable. Columbus himself distinguishes between "deceitful fancy" and "golden fancy" (p. 30). On the one hand, fancy has deceived him in provoking hopes for personal glory and happiness in a fundamentally tragic and disappointing universe. On the other, it is "golden" when it makes reasonable inferences about the future greatness of America and when Columbus blends it with the "memory" (p. 30) of his exploratory feats. Either way, it is answerable to reason. Freneau's excision of the most "fanciful" section of the poem, pictures II and III, from the 1795 version simply confirms the epistemological bias of the 1788 original.

At a pole opposite the voyager-wanderer Columbus in "The Pictures of Columbus" is the hermit of "The Hermit of Saba," which immediately follows "Columbus" in the 1788 *Works*. Columbus seeks new experience and knowledge; the hermit of Saba isolates himself in a wilderness where he hopes to be inaccessible to new experience and knowledge. Yet despite these differences—and this is Freneau's key point—their destinies are by implication inextricably interwoven. Columbus is the aggressor from the sea who is fated, however unwittingly, to destroy the innocence of land; the hermit is the passive recluse on land who is fated to be the sea-aggressor's victim. Like "Columbus," "The Hermit of Saba" is dramatic in form, its blank verse and somber ending also recalling Shakespearean tragedy. It consists of an unmistakably symbolic confrontation between the hermit and three sailors who are cast up on his otherwise uninhabited island during a hurricane and who repay his hospitality by murdering him in an imbecilic search for treasure they think he has buried in his cave. Although Freneau ends the poem with a heavily didactic and propagandistic four-line moral, the meanings he has embedded in the body of the poem are far more challenging, especially when considered in the context of "The Pictures of Columbus," than the anti-European, antiavarice ending suggests.

Between them, thus, "The Pictures of Columbus" and "The Hermit of Saba" define the tone and central theme of the 1788 *Works*. The tone is one of pessimism and a tragic sense of the circularity of human existence. The theme is that the archetypal adventurer-voyager at one extreme and the archetypal landsman-recluse at the other not only offer no answers to the riddle of life and death but endure a peculiarly futile, symbiotic relationship, the one feeding the other to no apparent purpose. Within this philosophical framework virtually all the other poems in the volume are meant to be read. Many of the most interesting of these had already been published—e.g., "The Indian Student," "The Lost Sailor," "May to April," "The Roguish Shoemaker," "The Wild Honey-Suckle," "St. Preux to Eloisa," "To Misfortune," "The Departure," and "The Indian Burying Ground." Although most of these were substantially the same in the 1788 *Works* as in the first versions, at least one underwent important change. "Port Royal" was transformed from a gloomy descriptive piece with symbolic overtones to as bleakly pessimistic and fully symbolic a poem as Freneau ever published.

The 1788 version of "Port Royal" follows the original fairly closely from the opening description of the tidal wave that innundated Port Royal in 1692 through the speaker's anguished outcry,

> *Where shall I go, what Lethe shall I find*
> *To drive these dark ideas from my mind!*[21]

In the 1786 version these lines are followed by eight lines of description, which end the poem. But in 1788 they are followed by a sixteen-line passage in which the speaker deplores a type of betrayal that recalls Sappho's situation in "The Monument to Phaon" and that reflects the pattern so often found in Freneau's land-sea poems. A young woman has been persuaded by a modern "Paris," as the speaker calls him, to elope with him and sail across the ocean to Port Royal, where he abandons her. Although Freneau does not identify the parties, it is clear from the final lines of the passage not only that they are his contemporaries but that the male is an ocean wanderer. Addressing the betrayed woman, the speaker asks rhetorically,

Are griefs like thine to Florio's [the betrayer's]
    bosom known?
Must these, alas, be ceaseless in your own?
Life is a dream—its varying shades I see,
But this base wanderer hardly dreams of thee.
                    (11. 99-102)

This assertion of life's flimsiness—that it is a "dream"—introduces the poem's twelve-line conclusion, which immediately follows the lines above. In it the speaker bids farewell to Port Royal with a statement so grim as fully to justify his outburst over the "dark ideas" preying on his mind. Port Royal is a place

Where Nature still the toils of art transcends—
In this dull spot *the fine delusion ends,*
Where burning sands are borne by every blast.
And these mean fabrics still bewail the past,
Where want, and death, and care, and grief reside,
And threatening moons advance the imperious tide. . . .
                    (11. 105-110)

What "fine delusion?" "Fine delusion" is all that is said, the inescapable inference being the delusion of the permanence, solidity, and beauty of the physical universe. Interpreted symbolically, as they were clearly meant to be, the lines convey a chillingly nihilistic import. Port Royal becomes an emblem of the fate of everything in the cosmos, the "imperious tide," controlled by indifferent natural forces, an emblem of inevitable universal destruction and relapse into chaos. All humankind's hopes to the contrary are a dream—a "fine delusion."

The poem's final four lines are equally bleak.

Ye stormy winds, awhile your wrath suspend,
Who leaves the land, a bottle, and a friend,
Quits this bright isle for yon' blue seas and sky,
Or even Port-Royal quits—without a sigh!
                    (11. 111-114)

As is often the case in Freneau's symbolic poems, the convoluted syntax here signals complexity of idea. Paraphrased, the lines form an ironic prayer: ocean winds, they plead, you need not inflict a hurricane on me to teach me wisdom when I sail, because I now leave the comforts and beauties of land fully acknowledging your and the ocean's tyrannical power over them, and I even leave Port Royal without a murmur of protest against your devastation of it. Yet the irony of petitioning and propitiating a force deaf to all petitions and propitiations is balanced by Freneau's commitment to ocean realism and his calm rejection of the delusory solaces of land. Although the poem exudes deep spiritual suffering, sometimes piercingly stated, its bitterness, as in these last lines, is moderated not only by the speaker's resignation to the facts of an apparently indifferent and inhuman universe but also by the steady rhythm of its heroic couplets and conventional poetic diction. Although deeply troubled, the 1788 "Port Royal" is a poem not of despair but, like so many others of the period, of stoic resignation.

Yet it does reveal the extremely dark cast of Freneau's thought in the 1788 *Works*. Most of the remaining poems in the collection oscillate between the thematic poles established in "The Pictures of Columbus" and "The Hermit of Saba." Although at least three that were previously unpublished — "The Man of Ninety," "The Misfortune of March," and "Philander and Lavinia" — etch the polarity sharply, the bitterest and most revealing new piece in the collection is in prose rather than verse. The seriousness of most of the poetry in the 1788 *Works* pervades the prose as well, especially that written from behind the Robert Slender mask. Although the tone of much of the Slender material is gay and good-humored on the surface, underneath it is often dark and cynical. Slender's "Idea of the Human Soul" is that it is like "a little wine or vinegar" causing "a varied temperament of the blood, and a different tone of the nerves"[22] — or, as the quotation from *The Tempest* at the beginning of the essay puts it, "such stuff/As dreams are made of; and our little life/Is rounded with a sleep" (p. 87). When a man drinks rum, Slender tells us, he learns the futility of pursuing any kind of happiness: "The moment he tastes of happiness it palls upon his appetite, and tells him, *I am still to be sought for.*"[23] Slender's sketches of various types of charac- ter—e.g., "The Market Man," "The Man in Business," "The Man Out of Business," "The Debtor," "The Private Tutor," and "A Visit to a Modern Great Man"—portray humankind as incurably selfish and bent on folly. The theme of selfishness saturates "The Bachelor's House" and "The Inexorable Cap- tain," which concludes with the grim moral that *"necessity alone renders one half of the world insensible to the miseries and wants of the other."*[24] But most chilling is the story Slender titles "Light, Summer Reading: which may possibly please such as have a true taste for modern Novels."

This strange, parabolic tale presents twenty uninterrupted pages of betrayal, deceit, madness, bigotry, and death genially presided over by a Caribbean gentleman identified only as wearing a white linen coat. The irony of the title seems to be directed not only at the contemporary sentimental novel but also at the assumed insensitivity of humankind in general and the story's readers in particular to the kinds of horror the tale proceeds to unfold. It opens with the discovery by Slender and the man in the white linen coat of a girl named Marcia, crazed at being rejected by a man who wrongly suspected her of want- ing to marry him for his money. Although Freneau seems to have based the story in part on his experiences in the Caribbean between 1776 and 1778, having Marcia, for example, describe a poem in terms that unmistakably identify it as Freneau's own "On a Lady's Singing Bird, a native of the Canary Islands, con- fined in a very small cage: Written in Bermuda, 1778,"[25] he transforms the experiences into grotesque parables and suffuses them with his mideighties pessimism.

This appears in the characterization of the man in the white linen coat, who is a good-natured but shallow optimist. When he finds that Marcia has been reading a poem "upon the *misery of man, the brevity and infelicity of life, and the certainty of death*" (p. 256), he blames it for having helped unbalance her and launches into a paean on the benevolence of nature. At his most eloquent moment, as he is praising the sun by saying that without it the cosmos "would appear to be fastened upon the shadows of death" and "all men and animals would inevitably sympathize with the horrid gloom," Freneau interrupts by having a poet, obviously a surrogate for Freneau himself, enter the garden where they are standing. The man in the white linen coat contemptuously tells Slender that the poet is "not only half mad himself, but is likewise extravagantly fond of mad people; and frequently sends verses to this same *Marcia*, which, most people think, serve only to increase her insanity." As a specimen of the poet's nonsense, the man in the white linen coat shows Slender the poem "To Marcia," published by Freneau a year and a half earlier in *The Freeman's Journal* under the title "Stanzas to a Young Lady in a Consumption." In changing the heroine's sickness from tuberculosis to insanity for the 1788 volume, Freneau hardly lessened its seriousness. Marcia, like the speaker of "The Vernal Ague," suffers from a *Weltschmerz* that causes her to cry out, as she watches seconds tick away on a clock, "*thus . . . shall verse decay;/And thus the world shall pass away!*"[26] Echoing "The Wild Honey-Suckle," Freneau equates Marcia's fate with that of a flower:

> *So drooping hangs the fading rose*
> *When summer sends the driving shower,*
> *So to the grave* Marcella *goes,*
> *Her whole duration but an hour:*
> *Who shall oppose the sad decree,*
> *Or what, fair maid, recover thee!*
> (11. 37-42)

In here applying the language of the final stanza of "The Wild Honey-Suckle" to a human being, Freneau seems to be clarifying the symbolic meaning of the earlier poem. If so, the honeysuckle resembles humankind in that neither is immortal. The spirit dies as completely as the flesh. "Duration" is only an hour between eternities of blankness. When in the final stanza the poet tells Marcia, "I learn philosophy from you" (1. 48), he affirms his belief that Marcia's view of the tragedy of her own existence, a view ironically linked to her madness, is correct.

It is the man in the white linen coat who is, by ironic contrast, deluded. Dismissing the poet's and Marcia's melancholy as a "perversion" (p. 260), he asserts that "It is impossible . . . for a thinking mind to be very unhappy at any time, or in any circumstances" (p. 261) and proceeds to praise virtually every aspect of fancy that Freneau had for a decade been denigrating. Fancy, or, as he terms it, "imagination," lays "brighter colours upon the gloomier scenes of life than strict reason has ever been known to deal in"; it "transfers every thing that happens in real life to the more agreeable landscapes of an inchanted and fictitious country" (p. 261). Identifying the man with a white linen coat would thus seem to imply that his is a mentality perfectly suited, like his lightweight coat, to the delusive Caribbean attitudes Freneau rejected in the 1786 version of "Santa Cruz." When subsequently the man in the white coat, Slender, and an Indian medicine man learn that Marcia has died and attend her funeral, they are upstaged once again by the "crack-brained" (p. 268) poet, who enters after an acidly satiric passage on the funeral services that the Indian and a bigoted Christian clergyman perform over Marcia's grave. His is literally the last word in the story—an epitaph in the form of an eight-line poem spoken by Marcia from her grave. Its chilling message contradicts everything the man in the white linen coat has said.

> '*You, who shall round this tomb your vigils keep,*
> *Wake me, wake me—I do not wish to sleep.*
> *My eyes were always pleasur'd with the day;*
> *Wake me, wake me, for here I dread to stay.*
> *In these dark shadows of our mother ground*
> *Where no sun-beam, or moon's pale ray is found,*
> *Nor gentle music bids poor Marcia weep,*
> *Wake me, wake me—I came not here to sleep.'*
>
> (p. 269)

The tragic tone of Marcia's epitaph is audible throughout the 1788 *Works*. Stemming chiefly from the conflict between sea-inspired destructiveness and land-inspired delusion defined in "The Pictures of Columbus" and "The Hermit of Saba," it strikes the volume's most somber note. A less bitter irony is found in the book's treatment of New England poetry. Freneau's attitude toward the New England epic was scornful, and it is chiefly to criticize the tendency of the New England writers of his day to write epics that he uses an anti-New England tone in the 1788 *Works*. The probability that he offered "The Pictures of Columbus," back-dated to a period well before the appearance of Barlow's "Vision of Columbus," as a corrective to Barlow's poem has already been suggested. But his main target was Timothy Dwight's *The Conquest of Canaan*, published in 1785.

The first unmistakable attack on Dwight occurs in Slender's essay "The City Poet," in which Slender and a friend, out for a walk, try unsuccessfully to avoid a poet named Menalcas and are forced to accompany him back to his miserable garret to hear him read from his latest work, an epic titled *The Fall of Adonibezek,* "*a poem, in twelve books,*" based on an episode "in the first chapter of the book of Judges." Freneau is obviously ridiculing the long-windedness of Dwight's rehashing of sparse material from the same scriptural text: Menalcas proudly boasts that "no other epic poem, that ever was attempted, has been erected upon so narrow a foundation as this."[27] Minutely analyzing Menalcas's treatment of the fact Adonibezek's toes were cut off by the Israelites, Freneau devastatingly parodies Dwight's poem for two pages, landing many blows on the New England clergy in passing. He concludes with the stinging comment, intended for Dwight, that Slender and his friend left Menalcas "not without admiring at the folly of a man, who, destitute of the least spark of poetical genius or harmony in his soul, was nevertheless attempting performances that in their nature as well as in their execution could only render him ridiculous" (p. 118).

Equally mordant but biographically more revealing is "The Fiddler's Farewell," a witty assessment of Freneau's artistic situation in the mideighties. In the poem, "Van Tweezle" is Dwight, the fiddler is Freneau, the fiddle is Freneau's poetry, and the villagers are the readers of American poetry. I quote it in full.

The Fiddler's Farewell

'To fiddle at frolics I find is in vain;
No creature alive will attend to my strain,
And I and my dog must be trudging again;
The strings of the fiddle
Are broke in the middle
Excepting the bass *which I never could bear,*
And to make a new purchase, I've nothing to spare.

The village all knew it, and car'd not a pin:
The night was so cold, and my coat was so thin
I shook like a leaf when the ladies came in;
They thought it a joke
That the fiddle was broke,
And never once offer'd my strings to repair,
But begg'd of Van Tweezle *to give them an air.*

Van Tweezle *began in so dismal a tone,*
All thought he had better have let it alone;
When the folks were to dance *they did nothing but* groan,
    Old captain O'Blunder
    Was brim-full of wonder,
And said, 'My dear boy, such a whining you keep,
You have hit on a tune that will set us to sleep.'

Yet, still he went on to our utter surprise,
And sung till the ladies had tears in their eyes,
And Bunyan *we thought, had returned in disguise:*
    We waited so long
    For the close of his song,
That most of us thought he would never conclude,
His muses were in such a musical mood.

Old ditties he sung that are fairly worn out;
The wars of the Jews, that were compass'd about,
Whom Titus, *the Roman, had put to the rout:*
    We all were in pain
    To be puzzled again,
For ten times before we had heard them, at least,
And far better told by the nurse and the priest.[28]

The need to be "trudging again" in the first stanza seems to allude to Freneau's decision to make a living in a nonliterary line of work after leaving *The Freeman's Journal* in 1783, and the reason given for this decision—the fact that all the fiddle strings are broken but the bass—is Freneau's humorous way of saying that his grim meditations of the mideighties have left him either unable or unwilling to write the trivia he knows he will have to in order to make a living by his pen. The idea that he does not like to play the bass string is interesting because, if true, it suggests the spiritual torment that accompanied the writing of the dark poems of this period. Exactly what Freneau means in the final line of stanza 1 and the opening lines of stanza 2, when he speaks about not having enough money to fix his fiddle and being laughed at by the villagers as a result, is obscure, despite its seemingly obvious reference to his literal shortage of money at the time. Within the framework of the fiddle-poetry metaphor, the fiddler's poverty suggests a poetic bankruptcy that Freneau—or at least his readers—may have felt he suffered as a result of the end of the war, to which he had devoted most of his poetic energies for years and on which he had built his literary reputation among American readers. This, or something close to it, seems to be the figure's central meaning, with the suggestion of personal economic hardship a secondary matter.

The idea that the broken fiddle is a metaphor for the loss of the subject matter that gained Freneau notoriety is supported by the final three stanzas, which in the main ridicule Diwght's *Conquest of Canaan*. The villagers' invitation to Van Tweezle to play for them hints of a shift in public mood away from Freneau and propagandists like him to different kinds of writers. Their wish to dance and frolic may be a metaphor for the public's wish to forget the war's unpleasantness and writers associated with it. If so, Freneau is obviously rubbing his hands together with glee over the storm of critical protest that greeted Dwight's epic. His jabbing at the poem's turgidity, its length, its allegorical pretentiousness (in the Bunyan remark), its didacticism, and its subject (the wars of the Jews) is merciless, as is the deliberate obfuscation of the historical setting of Dwight's poems in the Titus remark: Freneau insinuates that the poem is so unmemorable that the fiddler forgets it dealt with the wars of Joshua.

"The Fiddler's Farewell" is a topical and humorous version of "The Departure," each poem chronicling in its own way Freneau's leaving earlier pursuits and thoughts in the mideighties. That the two appear next to each other in the 1788 *Works* does not seem accidental. Although Freneau republished "The Fiddler's Farewell" once, in the 1795 *Poems*, he gutted it of personal significance by transforming it into a political attack on Washington's conservative administration in the early 1790s. Retitled "The Minstrel's Complaint," it metamorphoses Van Tweezle into "Ap-Shenkin," Freneau's collective name for his political enemies during the *National Gazette* period. The broken fiddle now belongs not to the speaker but to Ap-Shenkin. Moreover, Ap-Shenkin is both the feckless Van Tweezle and the fiddler. Although the result is a loss of virtually everything that makes the original poem interesting and effective, the 1795 version is valuable in that it clarifies, by contrast, Freneau's intention in the original.[29]

Freneau's controversies with New England and his broodings over the tragic relation between land and sea in the 1788 *Works* are of a piece. At the core, they are expressions of an inner turmoil provoked by the suspicion that human life and perhaps all nature is meaningless. New England's complacent religious orthodoxy especially irritated him. Having begun to doubt whether a deity or intelligent principle guided the universe, he found it increasingly hard to respect those who did, especially if they were political and literary enemies as well: they refused to hear the bass note he played concerning a universe potentially as anarchic as the sea and in which life and death fed on each other blindly. Yet he was by temperament unwilling to isolate himself from his fellow human beings and endure life in stoic silence. In less than two years, by the spring of 1790, he had left the sea, married, and reaffirmed the value of living.

V

"Tenacious of
the Shore," 1789-1790

For years Freneau had been publishing poems linking the ocean with maleness, the land with femaleness. Parts of "The Lost Adventurer," the 1786 version of "Santa Cruz," and the 1788 version of "Port Royal" portray men who desert women for freedom on the high seas. "St. Preux to Eloisa" uses the same formula to ridicule Rousseauian sentimentality. In "Philander and Lavinia" the female encourages her man's wanderlust and thus unwittingly sends him to his death at sea. "To Lydia" reverses the pattern by having the sailor urge the woman to sail with him and be his mistress. Central to these poems is the idea that, like the land, women are pretty and superficial, whereas the masculine ocean is awesomely deep.

One does not need psychoanalytic training to suspect that behind this antifemaleness lay intense subconscious pressures. It is in any case clear that after 1788 Freneau became increasingly involved with Eleanor Forman, finally marrying her April 15, 1790, and settling down to life on shore after six years at sea. Although no hard evidence corroborates it, W. Jay Mills's egregiously romanticized account of their courtship seems just reliable enough to establish that, as Mills contends, they wanted to marry in the early 1780s but were kept from doing so at the time by her family's doubts about the poet's finances.[1] Part of Freneau's reason for going to sea seems almost certainly to have been to change their minds, and it is possible that some of the pessimism of his mideighties poems stemmed from his disappointment both at not being able to marry Eleanor and at not making as much money at sea as he thought he needed to prove himself. Yet the relative scarcity of so-called courtship poems before 1789 and the relative deluge thereafter suggest that Freneau set his romance with Eleanor on the back burner until late 1788 and only then began to think seriously about marrying her. Moreover, a number of the poems, as we shall see, reveal strong misgivings about a sea-oriented man's tying himself down to a land-oriented woman, suggesting resistance on Freneau's part to committing himself not just to matrimony but to the whole spectrum of land values he had been challenging for a decade.

Yet by the beginning of 1791, as the poem titled "Neversink" reveals, Freneau had overcome his doubts. Gone was the bitter suspicion of and detachment from nature repeatedly voiced before 1789, replaced by a new conviction that nature and nature's God were rational, trustworthy, and wholesome. The contradictions in nature between life and death, creativeness and destructiveness, and order and chaos which Freneau had been symbolizing in terms of an irreconcilable strife between land and sea were now treated as complementary, rather than antagonistic, parts of a greater unity that required their apparent conflict for its own cosmic purposes.

The first unequivocal signal of this reconsideration of land appeared January 29, 1789, in the poem "To Cynthia," one of only three Freneau had published since the *Miscellaneous Works* and the first in seven months. Since the earlier two, "Modern Devotion" and "The Virtue of Tobacco," are ob-

viously trivial, "To Cynthia" emerges as an unusually clear
sign of a major shift in thought. The *Freeman's Journal* version
of the poem offers interesting corrboration of Mills's claim that
Freneau and Eleanor Forman had been in love since the early
eighties—if, of course, we are safe in assuming that "To Cynthia" was addressed to Eleanor, as seems likely from the fact
that Cynthia is identified as living in "Monmouth's groves."[2]
In stanza 4 the speaker complains he has been separated "too
long" (1. 13) from Cynthia. Nevertheless, he says in stanza 5
he "still" (1. 19) adores a miniature portrait she gave him in
the past. In the *Daily Advertiser* and all succeeding versions,
Freneau changed "too long" to "too far" and "still" to "half,"[3]
thus substituting spatial separation for the temporal separation
of the *Freeman's Journal* version. The revision is more noteworthy in that it is the only significant one Freneau made in
the poem for the *Daily Advertiser*.

Yet "To Cynthia" goes beyond the facts of Freneau's relation to Eleanor Forman to broader considerations of the relationship between land and sea. It opens with a pastoral image
of a stream in Monmouth that the speaker says charmed him
in the past but that now "Inspires no more my evening dream"
(1. 3). Although the speaker then applies the image to his separation from Cynthia by saying how "blest" (1. 5) the stream
is to be able to flow so close to her when he is so far away, he
ends stanza 2 with the familiar signal that the stream is "shallow" (1. 8). The hints here of disillusionment with the solid-
seeming land, echoing "The Vernal Ague" and "The Wild
Honey-Suckle," are reinforced in stanza 3: the "Shepherd's
moon . . . /No longer casts her varying shade" (11. 9-10);
the speaker no longer remembers what the birds sounded like
(11. 11-12). Stanza 4 makes Freneau's point clear:

> To me, alas! too long remov'd,
> What rapture, once, that music gave

> *Ere wandering yet from all I lov'd,*
> *I sought a deeper, drearier wave.*
>
> (11. 13-16)

The lines almost certainly refer to Freneau's entire seagoing career after his rejection by the Formans in 1783 or 1784 and beyond that to the whole process of disillusionment with land he simultaneously underwent.

What is new here is that Freneau now acknowledges a sufficiently strong attraction toward something on shore to force him, almost against his better judgment, to reconsider his position. The situation is further complicated, however, by his sense that he has profoundly changed since the early days of their romance. He seems to be warning Cynthia that his present love is no longer the pastoral, moonlight kind he evokes in the first four stanzas, altered as it has been by sobering intellectual experiences at sea. The ambiguousness of his feelings is subtly underlined in stanza 5, which introduces the portrait of Cynthia that the speaker "still" wears and that Cynthia herself hung "near [his] careless heart" (1. 20). The word "careless" holds the key to Freneau's meaning. At that time, before he went to sea, his heart was "careless"; now, by implication, he is weighed down not merely with the cares of commanding a ship but, more important, with a pessimistic, quasi-nihilistic world view that has affected and will continue to affect their relationship significantly.

The poem concludes with two stanzas that define the speaker's present situation.

> *Now fetter'd fast in icy fields*
> *In vain I loose the sleeping sail*
> *The frozen wave no longer yields*
> *And useless blows the favouring gale:*
>
> *Yet still in hopes of April showers*
> *And breezes moist with morning dew*

I pass the lingering, lazy hours
Reflecting on the spring—and you.
(11. 21-28)

These lines are ostensibly based on the fact, as we are told in
the title, that the poem was "written in Baltimore, in Maryland,
January 1789." Although Baltimore newspapers of the day cor-
roborate that the Patapsco River was frozen for a while in January that year,[4] everyone familiar with the Chesapeake Bay
knows that it has never ice-locked oceangoing vessels, powered
or sail, for an entire winter season. The speaker's suggestion
that he will have to wait for "April showers" to break up the
ice surrounding him is clearly figurative. On one level it is a
gallant exaggeration of his unhappiness at being separated from
Cynthia. More significantly, it seems to represent the initial
stages of a reevaluation of the stoic, pessimistic, ocean-oriented
philosophy that saturates the *Miscellaneous Works*. Psychological and philosophical paralysis, a frozen immobility of thought
and feeling, endless brooding on death—these, Freneau seems
to be saying, are what he has come to in the course of his voyage
on the oceans of speculation. A return philosophically to land
may, like the "April showers," bring spiritual renewal and re-
generation. In "reflecting" on Cynthia and the spring, the
speaker is engaging, as the word connotes, not in dreamy love-
fantasies but in a serious intellectual effort to decide whether or
not to commit himself to a land-oriented life he still perceives
as being "shallow" and delusive. To stay where he is is to remain
frozen in an intolerably harsh philosophy, yet at the same time,
as the first four stanzas of the poem argue, to return to land is to
pretend to reaccept values his whole experience on the sea has
taught him are hollow. Although he is "in hopes of" a change
of heart, he is warning Cynthia that he has not yet experienced
it and still remains locked in a world view alien to land.

The ambiguous tone of "To Cynthia" is also audible in the
next "courtship" poem Freneau published, "Lines Written at

Sea. Addressed to Miss _____, New Jersey." Appearing four
months after "To Cynthia" in the *Daily Advertiser* April 15,
1789, "Lines Written at Sea" was dated by Freneau as having
been written about a month before "To Cynthia," or "Dec. 10,
1788."[5] The most remarkable aspect of this poem is the fact
that although it makes fun of the "Margery" (1. 8) to whom
it is addressed in the April 15 version, saying for example her
"sun-burn't skin" is better than "Molasses" (11. 23-24) and
her "long projecting nose" is a charm "for which a thousand
lovers sigh" and "which while it lives, shall never die" (11. 36
and 39-40), its tone is completely serious in the wholly revised
version, titled "Polydore to Amanda," which Freneau published
two years later, February 10, 1791, in the same newspaper.
If we assume, as is virtually certain, the poem was addressed to
Eleanor, we might explain the revision on the grounds that
Freneau did not want the flippant personal references he had
made to a young woman in port in 1789 perpetuated when
she became his wife in 1790. The fact that the 1795 and 1809
editions follow the "Polydore to Amanda" version supports
such an explanation. Whatever Freneau's reasons for revision,
the self-consciously antisentimental original version remains
an obvious effort by the speaker to play down the seriousness
of his feelings for Margery. It suggests elements of the conflict
Freneau more soberly and maturely expresses in "To Cynthia,"
especially in the pose struck by its speaker of the unromantic,
roughly masculine, girl-in-every-port sailor. One way to protect
himself from emotional entanglement with this creature of
land was to treat her mockingly.

Still more indicative of Freneau's inner turmoil was the next
new poem he committed to print, "The Pilot of Hatteras,"
carried in the November 14, 1789, issue of the *Daily Advertiser.*
To clarify the meaning of this complex poem, it is helpful to
explain Freneau's general poetic treatment of the Hatteras region as well as his extraordinary use of it here. In general, Hat-

teras signifies neither the delusion nor the reality of benevolent nature but rather land stripped of its illusions. Resembling the mud bank of "A Moral Thought" and ruined Port Royal in this respect, it differs from them and similar images in other works because Freneau repeats it and gives it a consistent meaning in several poems. The 1787 version of the "Address to Misfortune," for example, presents Hatteras as the polar opposite of Caribbean islands like Santa Cruz, which Freneau uses after 1780 to connote the delusiveness of nature:

> *On* Hatteras' *cliffs who hopes to see*
> *The maiden fair, or orange tree,*
> *Awhile on hope may fondly lean*
> *Till sad experience blots the scene.*[6]

Similarly, the "Lines Written at Sea" that chide Margery treat "cloudy, sullen *Hatteras*, which restless raves,/Scorns all repose, and swells his weight of waves" (11. 29-30), as the reverse of the speaker's humorously sympathetic "dream" (1. 41) of Margery's nose. And in "Tormentina's Complaint" the female speaker, who lives on Hatteras, has been told by the ship captain to whom the poem is addressed that *"Hatteras Maidens are not fair"*[7] —a judgment the poem not only nowhere reverses but indeed underlines by giving the young woman the grotesque name Tormentina.

In other words, Hatteras carries antifemale connotations, and it is this antifemale tone that remains the most constant element in the three basic versions of "The Pilot of Hatteras." The first version is the most acidly contemptuous. Constructed, like the others, around an incident Freneau claims to have experienced in July 1789 off the Cape during a voyage to South Carolina, it recounts the attempt of an impoverished Hatteras pilot to get the job of piloting Freneau's ship through Ocracoke inlet, thirty miles southwest of the Cape, into Pamlico Sound. However, Freneau, the "wandering Bard" of all three versions[8] who is not bound to the Carolina coast but is merely waiting for the winds to change so he can sail on to Charleston, refuses the pilot's services. Into his account of the incident Freneau weaves a subtle attack on the denizens, male and female, of Hatteras. His description of the Cape as "bare and barren" (1. 5) in stanza 1 fits those who inhabit it: it perfectly portrays the pilot, who is "Content" (1. 14) with it because it is so poor not even pirates use it and because he can raise his flocks and bees in undisturbed "penury" (1. 19). That Freneau is mocking pastoral sentimentality seems clear, as does the irony of calling the pilot's existence "blest" (1. 17).

Indicative of Hatteras's physical and spiritual meagerness though the pilot himself is—managing the "tottering" (1. 26) sails of his "frail" pilot boat with fussily "busy hands" (11. 10-11)—his wife Marian is Freneau's main target. She stands on shore, "waving high her handerkerchief" to her "Commodore" (11. 27-28), as though he were setting out on a voyage round the world and not simply on another of his "tedious journeys" (1. 32) a few miles along the coast. Her emotional extravagance—she "grieves and fears" (1. 29) for her pilot—provokes these caustic lines:

> *Sad Nymph, thy sighs are half in vain,*
> *Restrain those idle fears—*
> *Can you, that should relieve his pain,*
> *Thus kill him with your tears!*
> *Can absence thus beget regard,*
> *Or does it only seem?—*
>
> (11. 33-38)

Questioning her faithfulness as well as her sincerity, Freneau pictures Marian as a nag who holds her man close to shore and to her circle of threadbare domesticities. In calling her a "Nymph" he underscores the contrast between the reality of the pilot's apron-strung existence on barren Hatteras and the Arcadian magic the word evokes.

The poem ends with a brutal image that reveals the truth of the couple's relationship beneath its pretensions of tears and waving handkerchiefs.

> *'Till eastern gales once more awake*
> *No danger shall be near;*
> *On yonder shoals the billows break,*
> *But leave us quiet here—*
> *With gills of rum and pints of gin,*
> *Again your lad shall land,*
> *And drink—till he and all his kin*
> *CAN NEITHER SIT NOR STAND.*
>
> (11. 41-48)

This scene of bestial drunkenness implies that the pilot can escape his wretched existence with Marian only through alcoholic stupefaction. Moreover, the phrase "all his kin" hints that Marian as well as all the other swains and nymphs on Hatteras take part in such debauches. That Freneau is on one level expressing his sense of superiority—social, intellectual, and moral—to the swinish inhabitants of Hatteras seems likely. More important, though, is the threat of entrapment on a female-dominated, morally bankrupt shore, which the whole setting and action of the poem symbolize. The pilot's very occupation connotes lack of freedom and imagination. Never venturing onto the main ocean, he clings to the shore, making pathetic, female-supervised gestures toward the open sea.

The coarse humor of this version of the poem, perhaps in part designed to appeal to the predominantly nautical readership of the *Daily Advertiser*,[9] seems also to reflect Freneau's uneasiness at the prospect of returning to land. The poem's harsh, baiting tone suggests a personal anger that he chose not to disavow for several years. The *National Gazette* version, published more than two years later, January 16, 1792, not only retains the first version's concluding stanza but adds two new stanzas that amplify the antipastoral and antifemale overtones

of the original. Between the second and third stanzas of the
original Freneau inserted a stanza describing in detail the pilot's
life on Hatteras. Virtually a parody of the shepherd on the
imaginary island in "The American Village," the pilot builds
his hut "In depths of woods," plants his garden "in the barren wilds," and enjoys his "wedded nymph, of sallow hue,"
whom "No mingled colours grace": "For her he toils, to her is
true,/The captive of her face" (11. 17-24). Marian's unnymph-
like character lies not only in her "sallow hue" but in the fact
that the pilot is now explicitly her "captive," a bondage consistent with Freneau's change of the word "Content" in stanza
2 to "Condemn'd" (1. 14).

This reinforcement of the entrapment theme is continued
in the second new stanza, which Freneau inserted just before
the final stanza of the original. Having in its first five lines introduced the idea that the speaker wants to console the pilot
with liquor for not being hired, Freneau concludes the stanza
with this sharp insult to Marian:

> *I'll give him half my store,*
> *Will he but half his skill employ*
> *To guard us from your shore.*
>
> (11. 54-56)

Since he has already made it plain that the captain has not hired
the pilot, Freneau is here alluding to future work the pilot
may get and, more metaphorically, to his own wish to avoid
the kind of confinement Marian represents. The reference to
"your shore" makes Marian, to whom the lines are addressed,
the symbolic proprietor-tyrant of the entire coast and the land
beyond it. In this second sense, the irony of the pilot's "skill"
in guarding Freneau from land is barbed: it is hardly the pilot's
skill but rather the wretchedness of his female-dominated existence that drives the speaker seaward.

For the 1795 *Poems* Freneau added still another new stanza,
which he inserted between the first and second stanzas of the

earlier versions, drastically revised the final stanza concerning the drinking binge, and changed Marian's name to Catharine. The new stanza is extremely revealing in that it shows the speaker brooding over the meaning of the land and sea as the poem opens:

> The dangerous shoal, that breaks the wave
> In columns to the sky;
> The tempests black, that hourly rave,
> Portend all danger nigh:
> Sad are my dreams on ocean's verge!
> The Atlantic round me flows,
> Upon whose ancient angry surge
> No traveller finds repose!
>
> (11. 9-16)

The speaker's sadness here is caused by his vision of the primordial ("ancient") restlessness and destructiveness of nature symbolized by the savage waterscape around him. Recalling the self-deceptive fancifulness of landsmen like the Indians in "The Indian Burying Ground," the word "dreams" suggests that the speaker is contemplating land and that the ocean is not merely forcing him to see these contemplations as insubstantial "dreams" but darkening his whole world view.

This sharpening of symbolic polarity between land and sea is explicit in the final stanza, which Freneau rewrote as follows:

> Should eastern gales once more awake,
> No saftey will be here: —
> Alack! I see the billows break,
> Wild tempests hovering near:
> Before the bellowing seas begin
> Their conflict with the land,
> Go, pilot, go — your Catharine join,
> That waits on yonder sand.
>
> (11. 65-72)

Gone is the crude image of drunkenness. In its place is as clear a signal of symbolic intent as Freneau published after "The American Village"—the "bellowing" seas in "conflict with the land." Yet the lines demonstrate a subtle shift in Freneau's weighting of the relative strength of the antagonists by 1795. The conflict is now between equals. Before, as in "The American Village" and "Port Royal," land tended to be devoured by the sea, just as death swallowed life, reality swallowed illusion, and chaos swallowed order. Now the land resists. To be sure, Freneau still patronizes and mocks Catharine and her pilot: aside from these two stanzas the poem is substantially the same one he published in 1792. Yet by excising the binge and adding serious treatment of his land-sea symbols, he frees the poem of its original tone of gratuitous personal pique and clarifies its central symbolic tensions. Catharine, the pilot, and Hatteras still merge into an image of the potentially scruffy facts of domestic life on shore, but now they are no more threatening than the ocean. The diminishment of the ocean in Freneau's mind by 1795 is suggested by the word "bellowing." Before, it simply destroyed; now it must try to scare with loud noises an opponent that is fully its match.

Yet the November 1789 version of "Hatteras" sharply opposes female land to male sea. How long Freneau, an artist whose personal life seems always to have been closely intertwined with his poetic symbols, could maintain such an opposition in face of his return to land and his marriage is a question answered by a revealing poem he published in the *Daily Advertiser* May 1, 1790, two weeks after he married Eleanor Forman. Leaving it untitled in the first version, he called the poem "Constantia" when he republished it in the *National Gazette* August 8, 1792, and in all subsequent editions. At first glance, "Constantia" appears to be nothing more than a clever joke—mere elegant froth. Yet in this forty-two-line effort Freneau outlined the philosophical compromise that was to govern the remaining forty years of his life.

The poem narrates an obviously metaphorical encounter between a young woman named Constantia, who has renounced the *beau monde*—she is "Sick of the world" and wants "to shun all balls and plays"[10] —and is getting ready to withdraw to a convent, and a sailor fresh from the ocean who tries to seduce her not merely from her plan but from the shore onto his ship. After fencing back and forth in the middle stanzas of the poem, they strike a bargain: for him she gives up chastity and her plan to become a recluse; for her he gives up the ocean.

> *What else was said we secret keep—*
> *The tar, grown fonder of the shore,*
> *Neglects his prospects on the deep,*
> *And she of Bethlehem talks no more;*
> *He slyly quits the coasting trade—*
> *She pities her—that dies a maid.*
>
> (11. 37-42)

The word "prospects," of course, has a double meaning. In addition to commercial gain, it denotes philosophical point of view. Earlier in the poem, Constantia counters one of the sailor's arguments with an amusing double entendre by telling him to go and "plough your gloomy sea" (1. 23), her insinuation being that if he does he will not plough her. The sea is not only "gloomy" but by implication sexually barren, making its philosophical "prospects" alluded to in the final stanza doubly poor. As Freneau had viewed it for a decade, the sea represented skepticism, pessimism, nihilism—a gloomy place indeed. In addition—and here we come to an idea that apparently crystallized in Freneau's mind between the publication of "Hatteras" in November 1789 and "Constantia" in May 1790—the masculinity of the ocean was not a procreative but rather a sterilizing force, both philosophically and sexually. This re-definition seems to have been inevitable, given Freneau's earlier symbolization of the ocean as the destructive and anarchic principle in nature. When after 1788 he more and more gave male qualities to it and female qualites to land, he painted himself into a metaphorical corner that led him inexorably to the idea that salt water was sterile and land was fecund. Indeed, hints of this formula are visible as early as "The American Vil-lage," in which the fresh and fructifying water of the idyllic island's semisacred fountain is "quickly in the salter ocean drown'd" (1. 114). Making room in his symbology for male fertility was a pressing need in spring 1790, one that led him to bring the sailor of "Constantia" to shore.

At the same time, however, "Constantia" argues that ascetic withdrawal from society to the kind of pastoral retreat Freneau idealized in the 1770s is equally barren. Although Constantia wants to go to "*Bethlehem's* walls" (1. 5), presumably to be-come a nun, her true motive resembles that of the hermit of Saba—to cut herself off from normal human life in order to commune with nature. Freneau underlines this point in the only major revision he made of the *Daily Advertiser* and *Na-tional Gazette* versions for the 1795 *Poems*, a new stanza in-serted between the second and third of the original. Says the sailor,

> 'The Druids' oak and hermits' pine
> 'Afford a gloomy, sad delight;
> 'But why that blush of health resign,
> 'The mingled tint of red and white?
> 'In cloister'd cells the flowers expire
> 'That, on the plain, all eyes admire.[11]

The "Druids' oak and hermits' pine" connote nature worship or at least withdrawal to the wilderness, and, like the "gloomy sea," theirs is a "gloomy, sad delight." In other words, the extremes represented by total commitment to a pessimistic ocean philosophy on the one hand and to an optimistic land philosophy on the other are as untenable in "Constantia" as they were in "The Pictures of Columbus" and "The Hermit of Saba." But instead of a sense of tragic conflict between the two poles, "Constantia" conveys a sense of the need for and the wisdom of achieving a good-humored compromise between them. The poem's witty tone is a sign of Freneau's hard-won moderation and mature thought. He refuses any longer to take himself too seriously and acknowledges that personal happiness in a baffling and contradictory universe requires compromise between conflicting extremes. Between a paganistic, druidic worship of nature and nihilistic alienation from it, he implies, lie the normalities of human life—marriage, child-rearing, social intercourse, the task of making a dependable living. It is this civilized norm lying between the open sea and the wilderness of land that "Constantia" informally celebrates.

It was during this period of intense reassessment between late 1789 and mid-1790 that Freneau completed the most ambitious treatment of land-sea symbols that he ever undertook. In a series of seven separate poems first published between February and June 1790 in the *City Gazette* and the *Daily Advertiser*, he gave a sample of what he said was a new poem, apparently epic in scope, that he hinted would soon be separately published. To be titled *The Rising Empire*, the poem was evidently to have offered a panorama of the character of the American people and to have outlined paths they might follow to future greatness. But it was never published. All that remain are the seven poems, six analyzing the character of six individual states or regions within states, the other, originally titled "Philosophical Sketch of America," giving an introductory overview of the rest. The word "Philosophical" in the title of the introductory poem is significant. The poem really is philosophical, not simply in its theories of terrestrial origins but, more important, in its establishment of land and sea as symbolic poles between which the analysis of particular regions in the other six poems is conducted. The seven *Rising Empire* poems, though fragmentary in terms of what Freneau must have had in mind for the finished work, represent the climacteric of his entire symbolic effort. They offer an indispensable key to his efforts to harmonize the land and sea after 1790, completing the process of giving male and female qualities to the two elements that he had begun years earlier.

Although the "Philosophical Sketch of America" was the third of the series to appear, it was clearly supposed to precede the rest, a supposition supported by the fact that in both the 1795 and 1809 editions it does so.[12] One of the most striking aspects of this introductory piece is that in defining America as the entire landmass of the western hemisphere, it allows Freneau to picture North and South America as an immense female island surrounded by the ocean and bearing on "her broad bosom"[13] all forms of life. Setting forth a theory of creation in which the continents arise from the ocean in a tremendous primordial cataclysm, the poem explains the changeful, inconsistent, and unstable elements in humankind's nature—the elements that drive human beings seaward as explorers, exploiters, or mere wanderers—in terms of aqueous origins (11. 17-18). That Freneau intends this primordial ocean to symbolize the nihilistic chaos that all his major sea poems of the eighties associate with the ocean is shown in his comment that the human race, "like the rest, from empty nothing came" (1. 21).

Although to this point the "Philosophical Sketch" seems to echo the skepticism of poems like "The Departure" and the 1788 "Port Royal," it subsequently makes repeated references to a superior creative intelligence that governs the ocean of natural chaos and forces it to be fruitful. Freneau speaks of "some creating flame" (1. 22) and of "some voice, that shook all nature's frame" (1. 11) and caused America to rise from the sea. He also praises "the great disposing power" (1. 25) and the "splendid power that cheers the earth and sky" (1. 39) and credits it with responsibility for humankind's progress from savagery to civilization. The "Philosophical Sketch," published a month before Freneau's wedding, reveals a fundamental change in philosophy. In subordinating both land and sea to a higher power, it resolves the conflict between them that had troubled him for years. Humankind's restlessness, internal disharmony, and impulse to destroy stem from a primal ancestor, the sea, as do the mutability and transience of the land. By creating land and life from the sea, the Creator implicitly decreed that both would, as particular objects, redissolve to nothingness. Yet the land and sea were inextricably bound together in the entire process of creation, representing neither absolute creativity nor absolute destructiveness. Beyond them lay the true seminal and destructive power of the universe, a reason that transcended all human understanding.

The six poems that comprise the rest of the *Rising Empire* sequence apply this land-sea polarity to particular regions of the United States with remarkable persistence and ingenuity. Each attempts to define the character of the people of a region in terms of proximity to and intercourse with the ocean and thereby to establish a complex psychological scale between maleness, ambition, restlessness, and freedom at the "ocean" end and femaleness, contentedness, quietus, and submissiveness at the "land" end. The most explicit of the six in these terms is "A View of Massachusetts," which appeared March 29 in the *Daily Advertiser* some three weeks after the "Philosophical Sketch" and which was dated by Freneau as having been completed "March 27." Freneau wastes no time getting to his central point. After four lines of praise for Massachusetts agriculture — a metaphor for the state's impulse toward an inland, peaceful, pastoral ethic — he moves at once to the heart of his interpretation of the Massachusetts character. The thirty lines

that follow shed so much light on the *Rising Empire* series as
to deserve full quotation.

> *Were this thy ALL, what happier state could be! —*
> *But avarice drives the native to the sea,*
> *Fictitious wants all thoughts of ease controul,*
> *Proud independence sways the aspiring soul,*
> *Midst foreign waves, a stranger to repose,*
> *Thro' the moist world the keen adventurer goes;*
> *Not India's seas restrain his daring sail,*
> *Far to the south he seeks the polar whale:*
> *From those vast* banks *where frequent tempests rave,*
> *And fogs eternal brood upon the wave,*
> *There (furl'd his sail) his daring hold he keeps,*
> *Drags from their depths the natives of those deeps;*
> *Then to some distant clime explores his way*
> *Bold avarice spurs him on — he must obey.*
>
> *Yet from such aims one great effect we trace*
> *That holds in happier bonds our restless race;*
> *Like some deep lake, by circling shores comprest,*
> *All nature tends to universal rest:*
> *Unfed by springs, that find some secret pass*
> *To mix their current with the mightier mass,*
> *Unmov'd by moons, that some strange impulse guides*
> *To move its waters, and propel its tides,*
> *Soon would that lake (a putrid nuisance grown,)*
> *Lose all its vigour, prais'd or priz'd by none:*
> *Thus, even base avarice helps to make us blest*
> *Not vainly planted in the human breast; —*
> *With her, AMBITION join'd; they proudly drive,*
> *Rule all our race, and keep the world alive.*
>
> (11. 5 -32)

The simile here of the inland lake is, first, an inversion of
the central image of the "Philosophical Sketch," in which, it

will be recalled, America is pictured as an island imprisoned by the ocean. Here, the shores of the lake imprison its water, the lake representing the fecund, passive, ultimately female immobility of that part of nature Freneau consistently links with land. Although he says "All nature tends to universal rest," it is clear from the passage as a whole, which details various counterbalancing types of natural motion, that "All nature" means the nature found symbolically on land. The invigorating forces of motion—e.g., "springs" and "tides"—are equivalent to the masculine drive to satisfy the lusts of avarice and ambition by going to sea: both have an unmistakably sexual connotation in which male aggressiveness and female passiveness merge to "keep the world alive." Moreover, the lake itself, however female and inert, consists of unstable water, suggesting its origin in oceanic upheaval. The result of Massachusetts's seaward urge is a "Proud independence" of character.

It was this independent, enterprising, "manly" spirit, Freneau argues in the final twenty-four lines of the poem, that was responsible for Massachusetts's leading role in the revolution. He finds the same spirit in Connecticut, but his "Description of Connecticut," published May 10, is less flattering than his "View of Massachusetts." Connecticut's soil is poor, the winters are harsh, and all citizens "bow to lucre, all are bent on gain."[14] Yet after twenty-eight lines of biting ridicule, Freneau begins an eight-line conciliatory conclusion with a two-line signal that sets his obvious dislike of Connecticut—a dislike stemming from religious and literary as well as political reasons—in perspective: "Yet brave in arms, of enterprizing soul,/They tempt old Neptune to the farthest pole . . ." (11. 29-30). Like Massachusetts, Connecticut has a masculine appetite for commerce and adventure that triumphed over Britain's threatened tyranny and made the colony "free" (1. 36).

The wittiest poem in the *Rising Empire* series is "A characteristic sketch of the Long Island Dutch," first published in the

City Gazette February 2 and reprinted in the *Daily Advertiser* March 4, which shows Freneau's alertness to the potential for humor in the land-sea symbolism of the series. He pictures the New York Dutch as an utterly pedestrian, unimaginative, parochial, and, predictably, female-dominated society. After broadly mocking their provincialism and fanatical practicality and cleanliness, he zeroes in on the image of the "strong ribb'd lass"[15] who, in her search for a mate, "heeds not valour, learning, wit, or birth,/Minds not the swain—but asks him what he's worth" (11. 25-26). Then, to show his amused scorn for Dutch manhood, Freneau pictures the now-married virago at the helm of the family boat on the way to market "While, plac'd a-head, subservient to her will,/*Hans* smokes his pipe, and wonders at her skill" (11. 31-32). This incisive vignette, with its comic reversal of Freneau's normal male-female equation, suggests that the Long Island Dutch have been "womanized" to the point of sacrificing all the ocean virtues to a stultifying domesticity and of making a symbolic mockery of seamanship. The poem ends with a tongue-in-cheek compliment to the "handsome Yorker" who, unlike her Dutch neighbors, "shades her lovely face,/ . . . Prefers the labours that her sex become,/ . . . And leaves to hardier man the ruder part" (11. 38, 40, and 42).

"A Description of Pennsylvania," which appeared in the March 17 issue of the *Daily Advertiser*, also defines a society in terms of its relationship to the sea. Here, however, the society is, as Freneau points out in the poem's opening line, "far from the main" (1. 1), with the result that it draws vigor not directly from the ocean but from the rivers that intersect it and carry its produce seaward. Freneau's exclusive concern with Pennsylvania's rivers in the geographical section of the poem —its first sixteen lines—is not accidental. Although he implies that Pennsylvania comes closer than either Massachusetts or

Connecticut to approximating a pastoral ideal of inland bounty removed from the fret and avarice of the ocean, he also implies that without its rivers giving access to the open sea it would stagnate and fester. These rivers are like the currents that freshen the figurative lake in "Massachusetts": their maleness is evidenced by the fact that the only personal pronoun Freneau attaches to any river in the entire passage is masculine (1. 6); they move through a Pennsylvania labeled with feminine pronouns throughout (11. 2, 3, 5, 21, 22, and 31). Fertilizing the land with their moisture and motion, the rivers are under the direct guidance of the "God of Nature" (1. 12) and represent the masculine ocean tamed to productive inland purposes.

The remainder of the poem, which consists of a ten-line tribute to William Penn followed by eighteen lines of general commentary on the Quakers, subtly reinforces these themes. Having three lines earlier established a forceful river-forest image of "mighty streams, thro' mighty forests led" (1. 14), Freneau introduces Penn not only as "wandering" like a river through forests but as a potent male force making a female Pennsylvania stop being "barren" and "bloom" (1. 19): god-like, he impregnates her "new" or virginal soil and transforms her into the fruitful matron she was meant to be, for which she "adores" (1. 20) him. Bland as the metaphor's tenor may seem, its vehicle suggests Olympian sexual prowess. Freneau picks up these hints three lines later by imaging Penn as the patriarchal Abraham of the colony who "beheld his tribes increase"(1. 23). Penn's benevolent masculinity not only fathered the state but "Bade virtue flourish" (1. 26).

"Pennsylvania" concludes with an eighteen-line evaluation of Pennsylvania Quakerism. It is significant that Freneau does not extend Penn's paternity to the Quakers, as one would expect. His chief point about the Quakers is that, "pacific in each aim" (1. 27) and

> *passive to a fault,*
> *They still are found, all complaisant to power*
> *To bow to ruffians in the trying hour.*
>
> (11. 42-44)

That Freneau meant his readers to link this passivity with the stagnation of the inland lake in "Massachusetts" and with the female torpor he associates with land throughout the *Rising Empire* poems seems clear. The Quakers, cut off from the moral vigor of the sea, represent a form of inland rot that even the ocean-flowing rivers of Pennsylvania cannot wholly prevent. Particularly interesting is Freneau's distaste for what he sees as the illusoriness of their religion. Repeatedly he suggests they are metaphysical dreamers, as when he remarks, "What tho' on visions they may place their trust,/I hold their general principles are just" (11. 37-38). This line of attack recalls the poems of the eighties, which express an ocean-oriented, stoic contempt for the illusions of land. Using the historically dubious tactic of separating Penn from the Quakers, Freneau absolves him of responsibility for their tepidly womanish attitudes. His dissatisfaction with the tactic is suggested by the fact that he omitted the entire Quaker passage from later editions.[16]

The opening four lines of "A Descriptive Sketch of Maryland," which appeared March 10 in the *Daily Advertiser*, are among the most intriguing of the *Rising Empire* sequence:

> *Torn from herself, where depths her soil divide*
> *And Chesapeake intrudes her angry tide,*
> *Gay Maryland attracts the wandering eye,*
> *A fertile region with a temperate sky. . . .*
>
> (11. 1-4)

In the 1795 and 1809 editions, however, Freneau changed the lines to read:

> *Lav'd by vast depths that swell on either side*
> *Where Chesapeake intrudes his midway tide,*

Gay Maryland attracts the admiring eye,
A fertile region with a temperate sky.[17]

In both versions, as the quotation from the first suggests, Maryland is personified as female throughout the poem. The fascinating revision of the Chesapeake's gender from female to male in line 2, the only one of its kind Freneau made in the series in later editions, indicates that the feminine pronoun in the original was a printer's error that Freneau corrected for the 1795 collection. If Freneau did intend the pronoun to be masculine in the 1790 version, his image of the female land being "Torn" apart by an "angry" male body of salt water is so sexually violent, so loaded with hints of rape and even disembowelment, as to explain why he subdued it, as he did, in the later version. Although toned down, the phallic image of Chesapeake Bay nonetheless received Freneau's approval in 1795. In no other way can his shift from the feminine to the masculine pronoun be satisfactorily explained.

Assuming that this opening image was meant to set a tone of sexual conflict between land and sea in Maryland, we can fully appreciate the rest of the poem's structure and argument. After eight introductory lines, it divides into sections of twenty-six and eighteen lines, the first analyzing the restless, ocean-oriented society of Baltimore, the second the isolated, land-oriented population scattered throughout the rest of the state. Freneau's strategy is to contrast these two groups in every way he can, with the result that the Baltimoreans emerge as caricatures of cosmopolitan, luxury-loving giddiness, the inlanders of leaden rusticity. The Baltimorean squanders wealth on imported luxuries; the inlander lives on "the product of his fields and trees" (1. 50). The Baltimorean is "Proud to be seen" (1. 25) at balls and banquets; the inlander lives in "solitude that still to dullness tends" (1. 37). The Baltimorean exhibits "Politest manners" (1. 19), the inlander "rustic forms" lacking "sprightly action" (1. 38). While from the Baltimorean "the

bright idea swells" (1. 24), the inlander "mopes o'er the evening fire" (1. 39), his "Meanest dish . . . his own discourse"
(1. 52). In Baltimore, the "blooming belle" flirts at all hours
with her "favorite swain"(1. 31);the inlander "bids the maiden
from the man retire" (1. 40) immediately after dinner. The
Baltimorean's home is a "gay dome" filled with "soft music"
(1. 21); the inlander's "lofty mansion/ . . . casts a mournful
view o'er neighboring lands" (11. 41-42). In Baltimore, even
religion "no gloomy garb assumes" (1. 29); in the country,
even wine "hardly makes [the sad master] gay" (1. 46). In all
this, Freneau's point is that the extremes represented by the
oceanlike Chesapeake's obtrusion upon the state are reflected
in the character of Maryland's citizens. Although finding some
good in both types, he concludes that their jarring natural environment exaggerates their activeness and sluggishness beyond
desirable norms.

The final poem in the sequence, "A Descriptive Sketch of
Virginia," appeared June 11 and was not only the longest but,
appropriately enough in terms of Freneau's apparent north-to-
south organization of the series, the southernmost in subject.
It depicts an almost wholly stagnant society, one so out of
touch with ocean influences that it not only condones but depends on human slavery. The chief evil of the institution, as
the poem presents it, is that it has sapped Virginians of moral
energy, destroying the spirit of freedom and enterprise found
among the sea-oriented communities of the north: "northern
plains more vigorous arts display";[18] Virginians are "Averse to
toil" and "rely/On the sad negro for the year's supply" (11.
27-28). Freneau begins and ends the poem by contrasting Virginia's original wholesomeness and vigor to the luxuriousness
and social corruption into which it has fallen. Although in the
beginning Virginia led the colonies in clearing land and build-
ing towns, "years, succeeding, see her efforts fail" (1. 6).

The passage in which Freneau symbolizes this moral condition in terms of land and sea occurs two-thirds of the way through the original *Daily Advertiser* version and, with greater effect, at the end of the 1795/1809 revision. It is one of the most tightly compressed figurative passages in the *Rising Empire* series.

> *Deep in their beds, as distant to their source*
> *Here many a river winds its wandering course:*
> *Proud of her bulky freight, thro' plains and woods*
> *Moves the tall ship majestic o'er the floods,*
> *Where* James's *strength the salter brine repells,*
> *Or, like a sea, the deep* Potowmack *swells—*
> *Yet here the sailor views with wondering eye*
> *Impoverish'd fields that near their margins lie,*
> *Mercantile towns where dullness holds her reign*
> *And boors, too lazy to manure the plain. . . .*
>
> (11. 49-58)

First, of course, Freneau is implicitly comparing Virginia's access to the sea with that of other inland states like Maryland and Pennsylvania and suggesting that, despite equal, perhaps superior, advantages in this respect, the state's culture is far less vital than theirs, a fact that amazes the "sailor," who represents the masculine vigor of the ocean. But the passage's imagery suggests more subtle meanings as well. Freneau does not follow the current of Virginia's rivers downward in their natural flow from source to ocean, as he does in every river image in "Pennsylvania," but reverses the movement by having the rivers wind upstream, "distant to their source." Just as "*James's* strength the salter brine repells," so all Virginia's rivers resist the ocean's influence—significantly, the sailor is imaged as working his way upstream against the current—despite the fact that like the Potomac they seem to "swell" to oceanic proportions. As the sailor probes inland, he finds the fields on either side of the river "impoverish'd" because Vir-

ginia's men have failed to "manure" them. Consciously or un-
consciously, Freneau is suggesting that the masculine principle
of the sea, symbolized as in "Pennsylvania" by rivers, has in
Virginia become impotent. Although the rivers "swell" im-
pressively—the word's connotations of tumescence here and
at other points in Freneau's poetry should not be laughed away
—they in fact resist the elemental maleness represented by the
sailor and the "salter brine" and cannot fertilize, metaphorically speaking, the female land. As in "Pennsylvania," the sexual
relationship between land and sea in "Virginia" is of course
purely metaphorical, linked as it is with the whole culture of
the state—its commerce, its intellectual life, its political, racial,
and moral values. What Virginia lacks more than any other
American state, according to Freneau, is the "manly" spirit of
the sea.

The culture of Virginia is the lake of "A View of Massachusetts" gone sour. Implicit in Freneau's symbolization of the
sea in the *Rising Empire* poems is the gradual change in his
thought traceable in the poems published after the 1788 *Works*.
Although the ocean still connotes primordial chaos and the
destructive aspects of nature, by mid-1790 it connotes the
creative potency of the male as well. Without the ocean as mate
and stimulant, the land stagnates. Both land and sea are gov-
erned by a higher power that harmonizes their apparent contradictions. Insofar as the sea continues to represent chaos,
nihilism, and death in the post-1788 poems, it does so within
the more comprehensive idea that life and death are at the core
complementary rather than antagonistic. In physical nature as
it really exists, the *Rising Empire* series implies, death not only
destroys nature but simultaneously fructifies and purifies it.
Without the decay and reabsorption of existing life into the
ocean of death, nature could not purge itself and make room
for new life, which in its turn emerges, as the "Philosophical
Sketch of America" implies, from that same ocean in an end-

less yet fruitful cycle. The vicious cycle of violence and illusion that permeates the *Miscellaneous Works* has been submerged in a broader plan.

Although Freneau had hinted at this philosophical compromise in two poems published in the *City Gazette* late in 1789[19] and more fully defined it, as we have seen, in "Constantia," he stated it with greatest elegance and force in the "Stanzas Written on the Hills of Neversink, near Sandy Hook, 1790," one of the half-dozen definitive poems of his career. First published in the *Daily Advertiser* January 26, 1791, "Neversink," as he titled it in the 1795 *Poems*, is the first unequivocal statement of his post-1788 commitment to a civilized norm lying between land and sea and his rejection of the extremes they represent. One of the poem's most remarkable differences from the poetry of the eighties is a joyfulness of tone established in the opening stanza:

> *These heights, the pride of all the coast,*
>   *What happy genius plann'd;*
> *Aspiring o'er the distant wave*
>   *That sinks the neighbouring land:*
> *These hills for solitude design'd,*
>   *This bold and broken shore,*
> *These haunts, impervious to the wind,*
> *Tall oaks, that to the tempest bend,*
>   *Half Druid, I adore!*

(11. 1-9)

Especially noteworthy is the speaker's compliment to Druidism in the last two lines, Freneau's earliest mention of the subject in his poetry. That Freneau, who had maintained a skeptical distance from religion in his poems to date, was by 1791 willing to identify himself with Druidism, however casually, requires some explanation. The webs of interpretation that had by 1790 been woven around the ancient cult were so tangled

as to be almost unsortable.[20] Druids had been used often by
English writers in the half-century before Freneau published
"Neversink," more often than not to represent a virtuous
primitivism in conflict with the vicious forces of civilization.
For example, Cowper's "Boadicea: An Ode," written in 1780,
pictures the Druid as a "hoary chief," "Sage beneath the spreading oak"[21] —in other words, as a patriarch in an age of sylvan
innocence. Much of the appeal of this image to freethinkers
of the century undoubtedly lay in their idea that the Druids
worshiped the same god of nature and believed in the same
religion of reason they did. John Toland established this interpretive line early in the century with his so-called *History of
the Druids*, actually three letters outlining the argument of a
history he did not live to write. In opposition to Toland, church-
men like William Cooke strove to prove that the Druids were
not nature-worshiping rationalists but rather the direct religious heirs of the Old-Testament Hebrews.[22]

Although we can only infer what Freneau's interpretation
of Druidism was when he wrote "Neversink," it seems likely
he was following the virtuously primitive, nature-worshiping
pattern laid out by freethinkers and that one of his aims was
to show disdain for orthodox Christianity by identifying himself with a pre-Christian, pagan cult. It also seems likely that,
like all other artists of the period who alluded to them, he
found the Druids useful as a vehicle for stating his own ideas.
In this sense the Druid functions like the Indian of his Indian
poems and essays. What he apparently represents in "Neversink" is Freneau's youthful wish to sympathize with nature.
The "Tall oaks" of the Neversink Hills symbolize the same
primal harmonies as the sacred groves of the visionary island
in "The American Village," and the hills themselves are designed for a "solitude" that leads to the romantic communion
with nature that Freneau idealized in the seventies, questioned
in the eighties, and now in the nineties employs with renewed

sympathy as a polar opposite of the sea. Plainly, Freneau views the Druid as a radical exemplar of this nature-worshiping impulse and here acknowledges his own wilderness impulses more openly than he had for a decade. But he is only "Half Druid." Although he says the forests of Neversink are "impervious to the wind"and their druidic oaks merely "to the tempest bend," immune as they are to the destructiveness of the sea, he cannot commit himself to them fully.

The topography of this stanza and the entire poem provides a symbolic rationale for the commitment that he feels he can make. In using the corrupt local name Neversink in place of the real and more widely known Indian name Navesink for the hills, he insinuates that this symbolic landmass, unlike the "American Village"island, Port Royal, and Hatteras, will never be washed away by the sea—will literally never sink. This is why Neversink is the "pride of all the coast." It symbolizes not only absolute resistance to the corrosive sea but also an intrinsic solidity and permanence Freneau had been denying the land for years. In "Aspiring o'er the distant wave/That sinks the neighbouring land," it perfectly fulfills the symbolic role Freneau assigns it. Anyone who has seen the Navesink range, a gentle, wooded ridge running north from Navesink Bay inside Sandy Hook for about four miles and rising no more than 200 feet above the beach, will appreciate the extent to which Freneau has exaggerated its natural features for symbolic effect.

In the second stanza, Freneau underlines Neversink's permanence by contrasting its timelessness with time measured in terms of human history. It has remained unchanged while various human societies, including that of the Indian, have come and gone; it has witnessed the revolutionary war; it has served as a reliable landmark since sailors first discovered its "towering crest" (1. 14) designed by the "happy genius" of stanza 1 to serve as a moral as well as a physical beacon. Furthermore, Neversink has woven itself into the emotional life of the voyagers who approach and leave it, giving "fresh joys" to those about to land and "a heavy heart" to those who are setting out (11. 16-17). Thus it signals the strength, permanence, and happiness of that area of normal human experience between the land and the sea, which Freneau identifies with civilized society and which in the *Rising Empire* poems he so carefully defines. The third stanza particularizes the argument of the second by tying the speaker's own experience of embarking "in search of care" (1. 21) and leaving "true bliss behind" (1. 22) to Neversink, which has watched him too trace his "tiresome road" (1. 24) over the "comfortless abode" (1. 27) of the ocean. Neversink has remained fixed while he has drifted, and he has come to identify it with the web of social and domestic felicities that he now terms "true bliss." One can measure the change in Freneau's attitude toward land since 1789 by comparing his view of life on shore under the shelter of Neversink with his acid portrait of the pilot and his wife in "Hatteras."

Yet the poem distinguishes this "true bliss" of shore life from the Neversink range itself. Wrapped in primeval, druidic wilderness, Neversink is the source, as the fourth stanza argues, of the "shaded springs of azure blue" (1. 28) water that flow down to human civilization below as a "luxury . . . to moisten CELIA'S lip" (11. 29 and 31). The water of these mountain springs resembles the fructifying rivers of "Pennsylvania" in that both serve as metaphors for the purity and vigor of a nature properly balanced between the male and female principles and for the moral refreshment a right-minded human civilization continually draws from that balance. The mysterious, primordial harmonies of Neversink are closed to humankind: its "rude retirements" are inhabited only by "deer" (1. 32), a symbol here and in several of Freneau's poems of an inaccessible natural harmony and innocence, and consist of

> *Dark groves—their tops in aether lost,*
> *Which, haunted still by Huddy's ghost,*
> *The trembling rustic flies.*
>
> (11. 34-36)

In other words, the hidden inner forces at work in these wild hills, though benign, elude humankind's grasp. Only the hermit-druid tries to grasp them, and Freneau has already told us he himself is only "Half Druid." The superstitious dread of the "trembling rustic," though misguided, is nonetheless more appropriate in its standoffishness toward the hills than are efforts to unlock their mysteries.

The poem's final stanza clarifies the speaker's compromise:

> *Proud heights! with pain so often seen,*
> *I quit your view no more,*
> *And see, unmov'd, the passing sail,*
> *Tenacious of the shore:*
> *Let those who pant for wealth or fame,*
> *Pursue the watry road,*
> *Soft sleep and ease, blest days and nights,*
> *And health, attend these favorite heights,*
> *Retirement's safe abode!*
>
> (11. 37-45)

Neversink, like virtually every wilderness landscape in Freneau's poetry, symbolizes the creative aspects of nature, communion with which requires the cessation of all human ambition and in its place the mindless impercipience of the vegetable and animal world. It represents a total and in human terms impossible withdrawal from normal human consciousness to the sentience of a wild honeysuckle. Yet beneath Neversink, on the flatlands lying symbolically between it and the ocean, lies the civilized "shore" to which Freneau now dedicates himself. Although the speaker cannot in a symbolic sense live on Neversink itself, he vows always to keep it in sight and to enjoy the land-oriented comforts that "attend" it. His vow to remain "Tenacious of the shore" represents not a rejection of the sea in favor of land but a compromise between them. The symbolic Neversink will remain Freneau's primary philosophical point of reference from this period on in the sense that it represents the renewal of his faith in the solidity of land and correspondingly in the trustworthiness of the benevolent impulse in nature. So strong is this faith that the threat of cosmic anarchy that characterizes the ocean in earlier poems practically disappears from "Neversink," replaced by the milder connotations of restlessness and striving for wealth and fame evoked in the final stanza. In its very name, Neversink denotes an indestructible, philosophical counterforce to the sea. Given the radical difference between these thoughts and those expressed in the poems of the eighties, is it surprising that the poem shimmers with joy?

VI

"And All Is Right," 1791-1815

The change in Freneau's private philosophy after 1788, as recorded in "Neversink," was accompanied by a change in subject matter and style of his poems visible as early as the *Rising Empire* sequence in spring 1790. Although symbolic rather than narrowly propagandistic in tone, the *Rising Empire* poems were nevertheless addressed to a large public audience and were intended to serve a nationalistic purpose. For the rest of his book-producing career Freneau not only maintained this public focus in his poetry but largely abandoned the earlier symbolic style in new poems he published. During the 1790s he channeled literary energies into newspaper editing and into writing poems saturated with a social and political reformism that was rooted at least partly in the increasingly optimistic and compromise-oriented private thought inspired by his marriage and return to land. Freneau's enthusiasm, for example, for the French Revolution, for Jefferson's social and political programs, and for the deistical principles of Paine's *Rights of Man* and *Age of Reason*, though consistent with many of his earlier political ideas, indicates a firmness of ideological commitment he was unwilling or unable to make between 1784 and 1790. Many of his post-1790 poems, dealing with such topical matters as dental hygiene and city shade trees, have a didactic, civic-minded ring to them missing from those of the middle and late eighties. Apparently convinced he had found a workable solution to the existential contradictions that had earlier perplexed him, he deliberately dedicated his talents to the public weal. After 1800, when he returned to sea for five years and then settled permanently in New Jersey, he continued writing this type of public poetry, especially during the War of 1812, and developed an increasingly explicit style in his private verse as well, openly philosophizing or allegorizing in meter. The few genuinely symbolic poems he did write invariably reflect the post-1788 compromise.

Change in Freneau's attitude toward the sea after 1788 is evident in the only nonpolitical poem he published between 1790 and 1795 that actually depicts a sea voyage. Appearing August 4, 1791, in the *Daily Advertiser* and titled "Minerva's Advice," it is a burlesque chronicle of Jason's first voyage in search of the Golden Fleece. Constructed around two conversations between classical deities and mortals—the first between Neptune and the poem's speaker, the second between Minerva and Jason—the poem opens with Neptune telling the speaker, who is watching the Argo's launching, that the Argonauts' jolly expectations about their upcoming voyage will be dashed as soon as they reach the open sea. Whispers Neptune,

> *'Bred up to sail on Meles' stream,*
> *'These wights at length would grow more wise;*
> *'The ocean has such waves, they deem,*
> *'As on that gentle river rise;*
> *'For songs and dances they prepare,*
> *'But fortune is the child of care.'*
>
> (11. 9-14)

The scene then shifts to the ocean, where Jason and his men

are enduring their first big storm. The helmsman has panicked, the "chaplain"—an anachronism Freneau uses to needle clergymen—has "left his cards and cup" (1. 21), the boatswain and the rest of the crew are stretched out on the deck, vomiting with seasickness, and Jason himself is "trembling" (1. 24). Minerva appears and scolds Jason for his "sighs and tears" (1. 25), telling him that "To honour, best, true courage steers,/ When thickest dangers round her throng" (11. 27-28) and that "Jove hates the wretch that's in the dumps,/But smiles on him that jogs the pumps" (11. 35-36). She concludes her divine message by advising him to stop his "sneaking prayers" (1. 39) and start handling the ship properly. "Rous'd" (1. 43), Jason "boldly fac[es] the stormy day" (1. 46) and brings the ship to land, where he ends the poem with "this wise remark" (1. 48):

> *Danger the ruffian never meets,*
> *As he grows saucy, she retreats!*

> (11. 49-50)

Wholly figurative, the poem presents Jason as the archetypal sailor-adventurer and his crudely amusing first voyage as an archetypal initiation into ocean realities. The bluff, salty tone of both deities and finally of Jason himself recalls the original version of "Hatteras," in which the experienced ocean voyager patronizes the naive landsman. Yet if Jason is the archetypal adventurer and Minerva the voice of practical wisdom, the lesson they teach—that ruffians win—is hardly one Freneau himself approved. After giving up the sea in 1790, Freneau wrote poem after poem in the nineties bitterly attacking the economic greed he felt was engulfing the moral life of the nation. The irony of calling Jason's concluding maxim a "wise remark" is clear, yet in having not one but two deities approve it he seems to be conceding that Jason's ruffianism—his lust for the punned-upon "GOLDEN FLEECE" (1. 30)—is an ugly fact decent human beings must learn to live with. Freneau here strips the ocean of virtually all its earlier philosophical over-tones and uses it instead to represent a bullyishness found wherever human beings scramble for wealth on land or on sea. Put another way, "Minerva's Advice" presents the obverse side of the sea virtues set forth in the *Rising Empire* poems: the spirit of independence that drives New Englanders to the sea and keeps them from stagnating into Virginialike lethargy can, if unchecked, lead to rampant Jasonism.

As though afraid of having overstated the case against the sea in "Minerva's Advice," Freneau published the rollicking "A Mistake Rectified" three months later in the *National Gazette*. Although the mistake to be rectified is ostensibly that of lands-men who look down on sailors, it is possible that Freneau wanted to reestablish the balance between land and sea that his new philosophy of compromise demanded and that he may have felt "Minerva's Advice" disturbed. After listing some of the hardships that landsmen attribute to life at sea—standing watch, exposure to ocean weather, bad food—the speaker, a persona named Sinbat used by Freneau in a number of sea poems, makes the further point that

> *Whoever is free,* he *[the sailor] must still be a slave,*
> Despotic is always the rule on the wave:
> *Not relish'd on water, your lads of the main*
> *Abhor the republican doctrines of PAINE,*
> *And each, like the Despot of Prussia, may say,*
> *That his crew has no right—but the* Right to obey.[1]

Surprisingly, these are the only lines Freneau ever published that contrast the authoritarian system of command aboard sailing vessels to the presumed democracy of land, a fact that suggests he tried to keep his land-sea symbolism as free of po-litically propagandistic overtones as possible. Here he has Sin-bat immediately refute the idea:

> *You'll say, its a prison, (by way of abusing)*
> *But, if its a prison—'tis of my own choosing—*

At sea I would rather have Neptune my jailor,
Than a lubber on shore, who despises a sailor.
Do you ask me what pleasure I find on the sea?
Why absence from land is a pleasure to me. . . .
(11. 33-38)

Although the poem defends life at sea throughout, its most revealing section is the conclusion, in which Sinbat suddenly concedes that, however unfair landsmen may be toward the sea, he would give it up if he could not make money from it:

Should I always be left in the rear of the race,
And this be forever—forever—the case,
Why, then—if the honest, plain truth I may tell,
I'd clew up my top-sails—and bid him farewell!
(11. 53-56)

Although the remark probably reflects one of Freneau's own motives for leaving the sea, it also suggests the nature of the compromise he had struck between it and the land. Transitions between the two elements need not be philosophically wrenching. The best attitude to take toward both is Sinbat's—relaxed, devil-may-care, able to be comfortable wherever you are. Sinbat's defense of the sea is as reasonable as his willingness to abandon it if necessary. Although "A Mistake Rectified" links the ocean with commerce and with making a living, it not only frees it from the stigma of Jasonism but grants it moral virtues as repectable as those of the land.

The most interesting phase of Freneau's career in politics — two years as the editor of the *National Gazette*—is among the least interesting poetically. Aside from "A Mistake Rectified" and "On the present state of Rivers," which appeared November 14, 1791, and February 23, 1792, respectively, all the new verse he published in the *Gazette* deals with public matters. Then, for fully a year and a half—between the demise of the *Gazette* in October 1793 and the publication of the *Poems Written between the Years 1768 & 1794* in April 1795—he published no new verse at all, though during this time he was apparently revising old poems and writing new ones for the upcoming collection. The 1795 *Poems*, which he himself printed, was a volume evidently designed to be his vehicle of communication with future generations of readers. Containing only a handful of new poems, none of major significance, the volume reveals Freneau's wish at the time to establish an authoritative canon.

First, it purports to define the chronological sequence in which the poems were written. So fictitious is this chronology, however, that to anyone who knows the poetry's real publishing history the volume's organizational pattern is at first baffling. Poems seem to be inserted at random, especially in the first half of the book, from throughout the twenty-seven-year span. It is only when the dates Freneau attaches to poems from time to time are inspected that his strategy becomes clear. The dates run in perfect sequence, with one or two minor exceptions, from 1768 to 1794 as the book progresses. We are meant to infer that all the undated poems, the great majority of those in the book, were written during the period defined by the dated poems preceding and succeeding each one. Thus, for example, all the poems placed between "The Rising Glory of America," which ends on page 46 and is dated 1771, and "The Pictures of Columbus," which begins on page 63 and is dated 1774, were presumably written between 1771 and 1774. The hollowness of this claim is especially obvious in the case of "Advice to the Ladies, Not to Neglect the Dentist" (p. 52), first published in the *National Gazette* September 29, 1792; "The Jug of Rum" (p. 61), first published in the *Daily Advertiser* February 1, 1791; and "Humanity and Ingratitude" (p. 54), first published in the *Freeman's Journal* December 8, 1784. Although there is no way to prove absolutely that Freneau could not have written at least a draft of the first two poems between 1771 and 1774, there is conclusive proof that "Hu-

manity and Ingratitude" could not have been written before
1780. The *Freeman's Journal* version of the poem admits,
without giving particulars, that it was "Translated from the
Mercure de France." The original French version, titled "Le
Noyé," appeared in the *Mercure de France* August 26, 1780.

The purpose of this rearrangement is plain. Inserting dozens
of post-1780 poems into the pre-1780 period and nudging
many others less radically into the past, Freneau redoubled
the effort of both the 1786 and 1788 editions to make it appear he had been a successful and productive poet since his
college days. Why he was so anxious to project this image is
not clear. Perhaps he wished to prove to those who may have
ridiculed his poeticizing when he was young that he all along
knew what he was doing, or perhaps he felt that the image of
youthful poet would appeal to his market. Whatever the reasons, it is revealing that by 1809 he had decided to abandon
the chronological assumptions of the canon he established in
1795. Although the 1809 edition is basically a reprinting of
the sequence in the 1795 *Poems* sprinkled with a score or so
of new poems, it not only omits most of the dates attached to
works in the earlier volume but splits the 1795 arrangement
into four books whose titles wholly erase the earlier chronological bias. Because in the 1809 edition he wanted to capitalize
on his connection with the Revolution, Freneau simply draped
around it the same sequence of poems he had arranged in allegedly chronological order in 1795.

By leaving most of the works in the 1795 *Poems* undated,
Freneau managed to suggest a chronology without committing
himself irrevocably to it, thus allowing readers who may have
known the facts of his literary career to draw their own conclusions about the book's organization. Yet one of the most important effects of the organization was achieved anyway. This
was the impression the book gives of emotional and intellectual
homogeneity. The poems of the ostensibly earlier periods seem

consistent in tone and thought with those later in the book, not only because many were in fact written late but because for the edition Freneau harmonized many of his important earlier poems with the attitudes and convictions he reached after 1788. In part this took the form of softening the argument of pessimistic and skeptical poems, especially those of the 1788 *Works*, and heightening their deistical overtones. It also took the form of generalizing and universalizing the mood of many poems, Freneau clarifying and focusing the symbolic elements in some and eliminating the personal elements from others. And it was also effected by his refining coarse material and diction from early versions. In other words, the volume tends to level the peaks and valleys of Freneau's poetic career which we have already surveyed and make it appear to be a smooth continuum of thought and feeling over the entire twenty-seven-year period.

Its tone is the reverse of that of the *Miscellaneous Works*. Confident, decorous, intellectually and emotionally serene, the volume strikes the note heard consistently in the handful of symbolic poems Freneau subsequently published. "Lines Written on A Passage from New-York to the Island of Madeira, Addressed to Calista on Shore," which appeared May 10, 1797, in *The Time-Piece and Literary Companion*, Freneau's final journalistic enterprise, expresses a grass-is-greener attitude reminiscent of Ralph's in "The Lost Adventurer." Now at sea, the sailor-speaker transforms life on land with Calista into a fantasy of Arcadian bliss. Yet Freneau's view of the fantasizing is sympathetic. The poem treats the sea not as a polar opposite of land but merely as one manifestation, however awesome, of a coherent universe. In saying nature "made not these abodes for MAN" (1. 69), Freneau attribtues physical and social discomfort rather than metaphysical horror to the ocean. Although he concludes with the equation between ocean voyaging and avarice that is a major ingredient of the Columbus-Saba polarity of the 1788 *Works*, he narrows it to mere moneymaking, stripping it of tragic overtones. And the poem as a whole tends to undercut even this mildly pejorative connotation. The speaker is, after all, apparently involved in ocean commerce himself, and his idealization of the shore is in large part, as the dramatic situation of the poem implies, provoked by the tedium of the voyage. We are meant to smile at and at the same time applaud his longing for home and hearth.

"Lines to Calista" is thus an analysis more of a particular psychological experience than of a broad philosophical problem. The poem symbolizes land and sea in social and psychological rather than metaphysical terms. It is in this respect similar to "Epitaph On a Sea Captain that Shot Himself," which appeared in the *Time-Piece* a month and a half later on June 26. Yet unlike "Lines to Calista," the "Epitaph," which Freneau retitled "Suicide: The Weakness of the Human Mind" for the 1809 edition, reveals his post-1790 tendency toward a more explicit symbolic method. The poem recounts the story of a suicide in terms of an extended metaphor comparing the suicide with a ship built by the "Shipwright, Nature," who "laid the keel/And gave proportions just and true" (11. 1-2). Ignoring his "feeble crew" (1. 13), presumably his family, the ship/man scuttles himself and swamps in midocean. Although its overt linking of the ocean with death recalls Freneau's earlier attitudes, the poem is far more straightforwardly didactic than his verse of the eighties. Designed to be understood by every reader, it outrightly condemns suicide, offering no moral — or literary — complexities. The poem's sharp focus on a single type of psychological abnormality tends, as in "Lines to Calista," to dilute its symbolic density. Its allegorical technique resembles that of later poems like "On a Fly, fluttering round a Candle," "Esperanza's March," and "The Brook of the Valley."[2]

Not all of Freneau's later symbolic efforts were so obvious. "Stanzas on South Carolina," "Stanzas Written at the Island of

Madeira in April last," "Stanzas Written at Oratava, in view of the Peak of Teneriffe, 1804," and "On the Peak of Pico, One of the Azores, or Western Islands" all resemble earlier work in terms of figurative richness. Yet they also reflect the profound change in his philosophy after 1788. "Stanzas on South Carolina" was published in the *New York Weekly Museum* in August 1801 and republished in the 1815 *Poems* under the title "On Arriving in South Carolina, 1798." One of Freneau's most impressive post-1790 poems, "South Carolina" is not only a magnificent tribute to a place and society he loved but also a careful, symbolic definition of humankind's place in the physical universe.

Asserting that the Carolina shores "Emerge with elegance and ease/From Neptune's briny main,"[3] the poem's opening stanza introduces the image that governs the rest: land sloping serenely upward and away from the ocean to more and more remote areas of "Sweet nature's wilderness" (1. 80). Although the next four stanzas pause to praise Carolina's landscape and citizens, the sixth returns to the motif of traveling inland from the sea to the symbolic wilderness of the mountains beyond the coastal settlements. Beginning with Charleston and the "half an ocean in her view" (1. 47), the poem moves landward through an agricultural region so bountiful that it seems a "Paradise restor'd" (1. 64) to a region, "distant from the sullen roar/Of ocean, bursting on the shore" (11. 73-74), of uninhabited mountains. What impresses the speaker most is the harmony between the mountain wilderness to the west and the ocean to the east, a harmony emblemized in stanza 13 by the rivers that originate in the western highlands and then, flowing east, gradually merge until their "force united finds the sea" (1. 102). The image of water flowing from land to sea, central, as we have seen, to two of *The Rising Empire* poems, here symbolizes the unity of nature and the harmony of its cycles. The ocean with its "sullen roar" once again connotes death; the inland wilderness, where streams are born and nature fecundates, connotes birth. Moreover, Freneau consistently personifies the rivers as masculine and associates the land through which they pass with the female deities Ceres and Flora (11. 59 and 62). Between the mountains and the ocean lies that middle ground of human felicity to which Freneau committed himself in "Neversink" and for which he finds an equally attractive symbol in the balanced civilization of South Carolina.

Yet in the poem's final stanza the speaker wistfully laments that despite South Carolina's charms he cannot live there. He says that if he owned "but a single acre" (1. 106) of this region "where such lofty scenes combine" (1. 105), he would give up all that had motivated him in the past — "cares that vex and joys that tire" (1. 110) — and never again wander. The stanza establishes ownership of land in South Carolina as a metaphor for humankind's wish to perpetuate the ravishing but transient joys of mortal life. Ownership of such joys is impossible, for human beings must die. Freneau's point is not that the ideal of civilized life symbolized by South Carolina is false but rather that it is impermanent. If in fact he could own the land, he would leave "all that men admire" (1. 109) for it, a vow that gives the Carolinian symbol genuine religious force. "All that men admire" implies religious worship as well as the pursuit of earthly happiness, so these "scenes" and the experience of living among them represent at least as great a spiritual value to Freneau as all other human faiths. Although the physical cosmos is stable and permanent, its creatures pass away. This uncertainty over humankind's immortal destiny, audible in many of Freneau's later poems, is almost the only echo the poems contain of the pessimism of the eighties.

"South Carolina" demonstrates that Freneau did not completely abandon his earlier symbolic style after 1790. A major impetus for a number of symbolic poems apparently written between 1802 and 1807 was his return to the sea as shipmaster during those years, the sea seeming always to have stirred his symbolic energies deeply. Two of these poems were published in July 1804 in the *City Gazette*. The first, "Stanzas Written at the Island of Madeira in April last, on the fatal and unprecedented torrents of water which collected from the Mountains, on the 9th of October, 1803, destroyed a considerable part of the city of Funchal, and damaged, to a great amount, several plantations, towns, and villages in that neighbourhood," uses the catastrophic storm and flood as a metaphor for the destructiveness of nature. However, though the ocean swallows up the human and nonhuman objects washed from the shore and in this sense connotes death and destruction, it is entirely passive: the primary destroyers are the island's rain-swollen streams. Land and sea blend in a single image of devastation. Freneau's aim in the poem is not to distinguish between the two but rather to define their united impact on the island's Roman Catholic faith. Mocking the "saintly tribes" of priests who "Forsook their Gods" during the storm and watched in "silent awe aghast,"[4] he argues, under the guise of recommendations for rebuilding the island, for a rejection of Christianity in favor of a religion of nature like that of the pagan Romans:

> *Who on this Valley's rugged bed*
> *Ere plans a street or builds again,*
> *Unthinking as the Brazen Head,*
> *Builds to posterity a pain —*
> *A Church, a Dome, that soon or late*
> *Must share the same, or a worse fate.*

> *Let some vast Bridge supply their place,*
> *Like those the romans rais'd of yore,*
> *Of strength — as firm as Nature's base,*
> *To vent the Deluge to the shore.*

Thus may the existing race engage
The thanks of a succeeding age.
(11. 97-108)

The revised version in the 1815 *Poems* underlines Freneau's metaphoric intention by substituting "Of architecture grand and bold"[5] for "To vent the deluge to the shore" in the second stanza just quoted, making the aqueduct image more general and suggestive. It is the poem's obvious anticlericalism and the symbolic suggestiveness of Freneau's description of the storm that define the aqueduct's figurative meaning. A rational understanding of nature would put an end not only to Christianity but to all supernatural religions. Although he concedes that the Madeira flood was unusually harsh, Freneau throughout implies that despite its violence the flood was nothing more than a natural phenomenon whose meaning was simply that nature destroys what it creates—such is the self-regulating economy of the cosmos. The aqueduct he proposes, of course, is the aqueduct of reason, by means of which human beings cannot only control nature but free themselves from the tyranny of superstition.

A similar sense of the inextricable interweaving of natural creation and destruction, without the anti-Christian overtones, informs "Stanzas Written at Oratava, in view of the Peak of Teneriffe, 1804," published a week later in the same newspaper. Here the volcanic peak on the island of Teneriffe serves as an image of the simlutaneous hospitality and hostility of nature toward humankind. Having in the opening stanza stressed that "Nature"[6] created the peak, Freneau first depicts its volcanic origin, during and for many years after which "man, ambitious, did not dare/To fix one habitation there" (11. 11-12) because of the "melted rocks" (1. 14) and "sheets of flame" (1. 15) that deluged "all that lay below" (1. 16). However, nature's beneficent counterforces have made the volcano bloom:

> *That plastic power, the solar ray,*
> *Descending showers, and evening dews,*
> *Have form'd a soil from slow decay,*
> *Whose herbage in profusion grows;*
>   *The stately palm, the unequal'd pine,*
>   *The dulcet cane, the generous vine.*
>
> *Upon the gaily verdant lawn*
> *The flowers a thousand sweets disperse,*
> *And pictures, there by nature drawn,*
> *Inspire some island poet's verse;*
>   *While streams through every valley rove,*
>   *To bless the garden and the grove.*
>
>   (11. 25-36)

Especially meaningful is the fact that the soil supporting this verdure has evolved from the "slow decay" of volcanic lava. From corruption has come new life. In the final stanza Freneau hints that the process may at some future moment be reversed again by another volcanic eruption and merely offers the hope that it will not happen in his own lifetime to his friends living in the peak's vicinity. The poem expresses both his acceptance of the interplay between life and death and his realization it will go on forever, after he and all people he knows are dead.

"On the Peak of Pico; One of the Azores, or Western Islands," first published in the 1815 *Poems*, returns to the volcanic image introduced in "Stanzas written at Oratava" and extracts from it further evidence of the harmony of land and sea. The opening lines of this highly compressed poem trace the water that fills Pico's volcanic cone to its source in rain clouds formed from the surrounding ocean. From the volcanic lake, the poem continues, water runs down the mountain, irrigating the entire island and making it "gay" with "verdure."[7] Simultaneously, the peak serves as a landmark to ships eighty miles at sea:

Long may you stand, the friendly mark,
  To those who sail afar,
The spot that guides the wandering barque,
  A second polar star.

(11. 21-24)

By associating its usefulness as a landmark with its cyclical
water supply, Freneau draws from the peak a double symbolic
meaning. First, it signifies the harmony of land and sea beneath
their apparent contradictions. Further, it signifies a cosmic
harmony toward which philosophical voyagers can confidently
chart their course. It is in this sense a "friendly mark" indeed,
truly a "second polar star."

But the central impulse of Freneau's nonpolitical poetry
after 1790 was perhaps best expressed in the score of philosophical poems he published in the 1809 and 1815 collections.
As mentioned earlier, the two-volume edition he put out in
1809 under the title *Poems Written and Published during the
American Revolutionary War* is little more than a slightly
pruned and revised reprinting of the 1795 edition which on
the whole follows the earlier volume's sequence of poems but
downplays its imposition of a fictitious chronology on the
canon. Its importance lies in three of its fifteen new poems—
"Science, Favourable to Virtue," "Reflections on the Constitution, or Frame of Nature," and "On the Powers of the Human Understanding." Grouped together at the end of the first
volume, the three constitute a body of verse unlike anything
Freneau had previously published. Unapologetically philosophical and didactic, they spell out as clearly as possible the
implications of the metaphysical system to which he had committed himself in the late eighties and early nineties. In them,
he does not joke, hide behind a mask, or tell a story. Their
central thesis, spelled out in "Reflections on the Constitution,
or Frame of Nature," is that from nature

> *. . . the reasoning, human soul,*
> *Infers an author of the whole:*
>
> *A power, that every blessing gives,*
> *Who through eternal ages lives,*
> *All space inhabits, space his throne,*
> *Spreads through all worlds, confined to none. . . .*[8]

So trustworthy is the reason by which humankind is enabled to infer this "author of the whole" that in "On the Powers of the Human Understanding" Freneau hypothesizes its cumulative movement toward the reason of the "author" himself:

> *Its knowledge grows by every change;*
> *Through science vast we see it range*
>   *That none may here acquire;*
> *The pause of death must come between*
> *And Nature gives another scene*
>   *More brilliant, to admire.*
>
> *Thus decomposed, or recombined,*
> *To slow perfection moves the mind*
>   *And may at last attain*
> *A nearer rank with that first cause*
> *Which distant, though it ever draws,*
>   *Unequalled must remain.*[9]

Although Freneau is tentative—reason only *"may* at last attain"such a status—his tone is nevertheless confident, buoyant, and optimistic, a far cry from the dark speculation of the eighties. He has at last located the communion with nature he idealized in the pastoral poems of the seventies. It lies not in the course of an individual's mortal or immortal existence but in the possible progress of the race toward perfect rationality. That such a doctrine is virtually indistinguishable from a deism out of fashion by 1809 suggests that Freneau put it forward precisely because he so deeply distrusted the romanticism of the early nineteenth century. Sympathetic communion with physical nature was for him no more possible at that time than it had been in the 1780s. He had tried and abandoned romanticism thirty years earlier; his post-1790 deism simply sanctioned the preference for reason over fancy we have seen him expressing since 1780. Humankind may in time approach the wisdom of the Supreme Being, not through faith in the delusive fancies of religious or romantic myth, but through rational understanding of the empirical universe.

The same type of poem is even more in evidence in Freneau's 1815 collection, the two-volume edition of pieces he had published or written since 1795 but had not included in the 1809 *Poems*. More than a dozen of the edition's 130-odd poems, under titles like "On Superstition," "On Happiness Resulting From Virtue," "On the Uniformity and Perfection of Nature," "On the Religion of Nature," and "Belief and Unbelief," restate or amplify the main points of those in the 1809 *Poems* in a similar style. They repeatedly invoke a Common-Sense empiricism similar, except for its hostility to supernaturalistic religion, to that which Freneau had heard from Witherspoon nearly half a century earlier. In "On Superstition," for example, Freneau asserts both that, "Implanted in the human breast,/ Religion means to make us blest"[10] and that "The reasoning power, celestial guest,/[is] The stamp upon the soul impress'd" (11. 29-30). Although Freneau's "Religion" here is a deistical religion of nature and reason, it is, no less than Witherspoon's common sense, a faculty or disposition preprogrammed by God in every human being. Moreover, it is, like Witherspoon's, profoundly moral: Freneau says, for instance, in "On the Religion of Nature" that it is "Born with ourselves" and "Inclines the tender mind to take/The path of right, fair nature's way."[11] And it is synonymous with empirical reason:

> *On mere belief no merit rests,*
> *As unbelief no guilt attests:*

> *Belief, if not absurd and blind,*
> *Is but conviction of the mind,*
>
> *Nor can conviction bind the heart*
> *Till evidence has done its part:*
> *And, when that evidence is clear,*
> *Belief is just, and truth is near.*
>
> *In evidence, belief is found;*
> *Without it, none are fairly bound*
> *To yield assent, or homage pay*
> *To what confederate worlds might say.*[12]

Witherspoon was convinced the empirical method would substantiate Christian revelation; Freneau was equally convinced it would substantiate a religion of natural revelation.

But the clearest measure these late philosophical poems contain of the brightening of Freneau's thought after 1788 is their insistence that nature is fundamentally stable and harmonious. Arguing, like Paine's *Age of Reason*, that the physical universe is God's sole revelation to humankind and that all moral knowledge comes from it, these new poems, like those Freneau had published in 1809, insist that in obeying perfectly uniform laws nature exhibits the rationality and perfection of the Creator himself. Accordingly, nature demonstrates to the rational mind the essential rightness, fitness, and goodness of all natural phenomena, including death. Echoing the conclusion of the first epistle of Pope's *Essay on Man*, published almost a century earlier, Freneau argues at the end of "On the Uniformity and Perfection of Nature" that

> *No imperfection can be found*
> *In all that is, above, around, —*
> *All, nature made, in reason's sight*
> *Is order all, and all is right.*[13]

Altogether abandoning symbolism in favor of direct statement of his ideas, Freneau in these poems expressed the central faith underlying all his poems after 1790: nature did not, as he once feared, war with itself.

VII

Conclusion

Freneau's championing of deism late in life was the final phase of a complex process of intellectual and artistic development. As a young man, he romanticized nature; only after 1780 did he begin eyeing it with the corrosive skepticism that led him by the mideighties to the verge of rationalistic despair. His "conversion" to deism between 1788 and 1790 was largely a stepping-back from the nihilistic materialism his rationalism had been drawing him toward. He returned to nature after 1790, cured, however, not only of the romantic fancy that had originally drawn him to it in the 1770s but also of the skepticism that had nearly ruined it for him a decade later. His development as a poet closely paralleled these developments in thought. During the seventies he tended to write long, rambling poems that praised the power of fancy to rise above the mundane. Around 1780, however, he adopted a pithy, compressed style in his best lyrics that allowed him to get quickly to the marrow of his thought. His use of a consistent symbology not merely of land and sea but of heat and cold, light and dark, calm and storm, and summer and winter was both efficient and appropriate to his harshly realistic assessment of life.

After 1790 he largely abandoned private symbolism for more public modes of expression and in effect ended his career teaching the consolations of deistic philosophy.

Although most of Freneau's major sea poems were written before the romanticization of the sea which took place during the first half of the nineteenth century, the art that he produced during the most impressive decade of his literary career is closer in spirit to Herman Melville's than to that of any American sea-writer who stands between them chronologically. Like Melville, Freneau transformed experience as a professional sailor into a symbolism that imaged the ocean as the unknown and the ocean voyage as the quest for metaphysical knowledge. Further, he and Melville both pictured land as a safe and superficial contrast to the bottomless sea, which they associated with a potential nihilism most of their contemporaries refused to acknowledge. Each was hostile to the romanticism of his age. Each rejected his Calvinistic heritage in favor of a thoroughgoing skepticism. Each adopted an oblique and covert style that contemporary readers never penetrated. James Fenimore Cooper achieved the symbolic depth and consistency of neither writer, and his last sea novel, *The Sea Lions* (1849), was more aggressively Christian than his first, *The Pilot* (1824). Also, despite some muting of the romanticism of his early work, Cooper remained an unmistakably romantic sea-writer to the end. Poe's *Arthur Gordon Pym* (1838) is a masterpiece of adventure entertainment, Dana's *Two Years Before the Mast* (1840) a masterpiece of descriptive autobiography. Neither is symbolically or philosophically complex.

Any similarity between Freneau and Melville must, of course, be kept in perspective. There is no evidence Melville ever read Freneau, much less understood what he was attempting in poems like "The Hurricane" and "The Departure." Freneau wrote before Byron, Cooper, and others had transformed the ocean from the antisocial chaos that it had been since classical times into the arena of sublime self-fulfillment that it had become by Melville's day. After 1790, Freneau espoused an optimistic deism that was light years distant, philosophically speaking, from the uncompromisingly pessimistic agnosticism of Melville's post-Civil War poetry. Yet the fact remains that during one decade of his life Freneau produced a body of writing strikingly anticipatory of central themes and methods Melville was to use more than fifty years later. Like Melville, he was one of the most thoughtful, independent, and original artists of his period. As the author of at least a hundred poems whose inner meanings have gone all but unnoticed for two centuries, he should begin to be recognized for what he is: one of America's genuinely important poets.

NOTES

Notes

CHAPTER I

1. "Introduction," *Poems of Freneau* (New York: Hafner Publishing, 1968), p. liv.

2. The foregoing sketch is a synthesis of the five major biographies of Freneau: Mary S. Austin, *Philip Freneau: The Poet of the Revolution* (New York: A. Wessels, 1901); Fred Lewis Pattee, "Life of Philip Freneau," *The Poems of Philip Freneau*, 3 vols. (Princeton: Princeton University Press, 1902-1907), I, xiii-cxii; Lewis Leary, *That Rascal Freneau: A Study in Literary Failure* (New Brunswick: Rutgers University Press, 1941); Jacob Axelrad, *Philip Freneau: Champion of Democracy* (Austin, University of Texas Press, 1967); and Philip M. Marsh, *Philip Freneau: Poet and Journalist* (Minneapolis: Dillon Press, 1967).

3. Pattee, *Poems of Freneau*, I, p. cviii.

4. *Ibid.*

5. *Ibid.*, p. lxix.

6. *Ibid.*, p. xcvi.

7. *Ibid.*, pp. xxxviii, civ.

8. Clark, *Poems of Freneau*, p. liv.

9. *Ibid.*

10. *Ibid.*, p. lv.

11. *Ibid.*

12. Leary, *That Rascal Freneau*, p. ix.

13. *Ibid.*, p. 29.

14. *Ibid.*

15. *Ibid.*, p. ix.

16. *Ibid.*, p. 345.

17. (New York: New York University Press, 1949), p. 4.

18. *Ibid.*, p. 80.

19. *Ibid.*, pp. 80, 81.

20. *Ibid.*, p. 81.

21. Axelrad, p. 357.

22. *Ibid.*, p. 338.

23. *Ibid.*, p. 371.

24. Marsh, *Freneau*, p. 1.

25. *Ibid.*, p. iii.

26. *The Works of Philip Freneau: A Critical Study* (Metuchen, N.J.: Scarecrow Press, 1968), p. 181.

27. *Philip Freneau* (Boston: Twayne Publishers, 1976), p. 10.

28. *Ibid.*, p. 171.

29. *Ibid.*, p. 156.

30. *Johns Hopkins University Studies*, XX (1902), 1-105.

31. *James Fenimore Cooper and the Development of American Sea Fiction* (Cambridge: Harvard University Press, 1961), pp. 18, 20.

32. *The Lay of the Land: Metaphor as Experience and History in American Life and Letters* (Chapel Hill: University of North Carolina Press, 1975), p. 30.

33. Roger B. Stein, *Seascape and the American Imagination* (New York: Clarkson N. Potter, 1975), pp. 12, 20; W. H. Auden, *The Enchafed Flood: or The Romantic Iconography of the Sea* (New York: Random House, 1950), pp. 7-14.

34. See Roger B. Stein, "Seascape and the American Imagination: The Puritan Seventeenth Century," *Early American Literature*, VI (1972-73), 17-37, and Sacvan Bercovitch, *The Puritan Origins of the American Self* (New Haven: Yale University Press, 1975), pp. 117-20.

35. See Roger B. Stein, "Copley's *Watson and the Shark* and Aesthetics in the 1770s," *Discoveries and Considerations: Essays on Early American Literature and Aesthetics Presented to Harold Jantz* (Albany: State University of New York Press, 1976), pp. 85-130, and "Pulled Out of the Bay: American Fiction in the Eighteenth Century," *Studies in American Fiction*, II (1974), 13-36.

36. Chester F. Chapin, *Personification in Eighteenth-Century English Poetry* (New York: Columbia University Press, 1955); Patricia Meyer Spacks, *The Poetry of Vision: Five Eighteenth-Century Poets* (Cambridge: Harvard University Press, 1967); Paul Fussell, *The Rhetorical World of Augustan Humanism: Ethics and Imagery from Swift to Burke* (Oxford: Oxford University Press, 1965); and Cecil V. Deane, *Aspects of Eighteenth Century Nature Poetry* (London: Frank Cass, 1967).

37. Studies stressing Freneau's imitation of earlier poets include Harry Hayden Clark, "The Literary Influences of Philip Freneau," *Studies in Philology*, XXII (1925), 1-33; Joseph M. Beatty, Jr., "Churchill and Freneau," *American Literature*, II (1930), 121-30; V. E. Gibbens, "A Note on Three Lyrics of Philip Freneau, and Their Similarity to Collins' Poems," *Modern Language Notes*, LIX (1944), 313-15; and Thomas P. Haviland, "A Measure of the Early Freneau's Debt to Milton," *Publications of the Modern Language Association*, LV (1940), 1033-40. See also Leary, *That Rascal Freneau*, pp. 21-33, 39-45.

38. Meyer H. Abrams, *The Mirror and the Lamp: Romantic Theory and the Critical Tradition* (New York: Norton, 1958), pp. 3-29.

39. The definitive study of the entire controversy is Alan Heimert, *Religion*

and the American Mind from the Great Awakening to the Revolution (Cambridge: Harvard University Press, 1966). See also Herbert W. Schneider, *The Puritan Mind* (Ann Arbor: University of Michigan Press, 1958); Bercovitch, *Puritan Origins*; and Douglas Sloan, *The Scottish Enlightenment and the American College Ideal* (New York: Teachers College Press, Columbia University, 1971).

40. Sloan, *Scottish Enlightment*, pp. 101-45.

41. *Ibid.*, pp. 122-25.

42. Freneau's manuscript notebook, as quoted in Leary, *That Rascal Freneau*, p. 49.

43. Freneau's awareness of typology—the discovering of events called antitypes in the New Testament which fulfilled their types, or foreshadowings, in the Old— is evidenced by the references he makes to it in his poetry. For example, in the 1779 version of "The House of Night," he alludes to "New Jordan's stream prefigured by the old" (*The United States Magazine*, I [1779], p. 362, l. 282); in 1782 he makes a complex and witty series of puns on Bible types and printer's types in the "Epigram occasioned by the Title of Rivington's Royal Gazette being scarcely legible" (*The Freeman's Journal* [February 13, 1782]); and in the 1786 version of "The Beauties of Santa Cruz" he compares North Americans hesitating to come to the Caribbean with the Israelites looking over Jordan at "Heav'ns type in view, the canaanitish green" (*The Poems of Philip Freneau Written Chiefly during the Late War* [Philadelphia: Francis Bailey, 1786], pp. 133-52, l. 20).

44. "Copley's *Watson and the Shark,*" *Discoveries and Considerations*, pp. 85-130.

45. *Ibid.*, p. 104.

CHAPTER II

1. "The American Village," *The American Village, A Poem. To which are added, Several Other Original Pieces in Verse* (New York: Burt Franklin, 1968), pp. 1-18, l. 88.

2. *A Cultural History of the American Revolution* (New York: Thomas Y. Crowell, 1976), p. 304.

3. Kolodny, *Lay of the Land*, pp. 33-37, and William L. Andrews, "Goldsmith and Freneau in 'The American Village,'" *Early American Literature* V, No. 2 (1970), 14-23d, have offered the only challenges to the Clark-Leary view that "The American Village" is wholly derivative, Kolodny arguing that the poem sets forth a double pastoral vision of America, Andrews that although the poem opens on a public note it becomes introspective in the island passage and continues so to the end.

4. Freneau to Madison, November 22, 1772, *Prose Works*, p. 475.

5. *The American Village*, pp. 19-22, l. 15.

6. Edith Hamilton, *Mythology* (New York: The New American Library, 1959), p. 116.

7. The influence of classical thought and literature on Freneau is well known. See especially Ruth W. Brown, "Classical Echoes in the Poetry of Philip Freneau," *The Classical Journal*, XLV (1949-50), 29-34, and Adkins, *Cosmic Enigma*, pp. 57-79.

8. *The United States Magazine* I (1779), 355-363, ll. 11 and 25. The 1779 version is reprinted as an appendix in Lewis Leary, "The Dream Visions of Philip Freneau," *Early American Literature*, XI (1976-77), 156-82.

9. See lines 14, 27, 51, and 278.

10. *U.S. Magazine* I (February 1779), pp. 81-88.

11. *Ibid.*, p. 84.

12. *That Rascal Freneau*, p. 70.

13. The text of the 1772 edition is given in Pattee, I, 49-84 *n*.

14. *U.S. Magazine* I (June 1779), pp. 282-83, ll. 5-24.

15. *Ibid.*, pp. 281-82.

16. Silverman, *A Cultural History of the American Revolution*, p. 305.

17. *The Oxford Classical Dictionary*, Second Edition (London: Oxford University Press, 1970), p. 1091.

18. *The Aenid of Virgil*, trans. by C. Day Lewis (New York: Doubleday, 1956), p. 138.

CHAPTER III

1. Freneau's marginalia, *Miscellanies for Sentimentalists* (Philadelphia: Robert Bell, 1778), p. 4 of the Rochefoucault section. Copy in Rutgers University Library.

2. See, for example, Pattee, I, xxxiii-xxxiv; Clark, *Poems of Freneau*, pp. xviii-xix; Leary, pp. 83-84; Axelrad, pp. 110-111; and Marsh, *Freneau*, pp. 71-72.

3. *The British Prison-Ship: A Poem, in Four Cantoes* (Philadelphia: Francis Bailey, 1781), pp. 19-20.

4. "On the fall of general earl Cornwallis . . . ," *The Freeman's Journal* (November 7, 1781), ll. 195-202.

5. *Ibid.* (October 24, 1781), ll. 9-16.

6. *Ibid.* (January 2, 1782), ll. 17-22.

7. Pp. 77-78 and *passim*.

8. *The Freeman's Journal* (March 17, 1784), l. 52.

9. *Ibid.* (November 21, 1781), l. 11.

10. *Ibid.* (July 17, 1782), ll. 27-28.

11. *Ibid.* (March 23, 1785), ll. 13-16.

12. Marsh, *Works of Freneau*, pp. 39-45.

13. "The Pilgrim, No. XII," *The Freeman's Journal* (February 13, 1782).

14. *Ibid.* (April 13, 1785), ll. 1-12.

15. Adkins's exposition, *Cosmic Enigma*, pp. 61-72, of Freneau's debt to Lucretian materialism provides a possible source for the nihilistic overtones not only of "The Hurricane" but of many other poems Freneau published during the eighties. Although Freneau seems to have reached his conclusions largely independent of sources, he nevertheless seems, as Adkins argues, to have been strongly drawn to Lucretian thought.

16. *The Freeman's Journal* (May 18, 1785), ll. 21-28.

17. Compare *The Freeman's Journal* (May 25, 1785); *The Poems of Philip Freneau* (Philadelphia: Francis Bailey, 1786), pp. 18-20; and *Poems Written between the years 1768 & 1794, by Philip Freneau* (Mt. Pleasant: Philip Freneau, 1795), pp. 30-31.

18. *The Columbian Herald: or the Independent Courier of North America* (February 2, 1786), l. 6.

19. *Cooper and the Development of American Sea Fiction* pp. 18-19.

20. *The Columbian Herald* (March 6, 1786), l. 1.

21. "The Lost Sailor," *Works* (1788), pp. 74-75, ll. 14-18.

22. *Poems* (1786), p. viii.

23. *Ibid.*, pp. 32-34.

24. See, for example, Axelrad, pp. 27-28, and Leary, *That Rascal Freneau*, pp. 28-30.

25. *Poems* (1786), pp. 23-27, l. 7.

26. *Poems* (1795), pp. 31-32, and 372-74. Bowden, *Philip Freneau*, describes the revisions on pages 133-34 of her book.

27. *United States Magazine*, p. 361, ll. 209-28.

28. *Poems* (1786), pp. 101-23, l. 437.

29. *United States Magazine*, ll. 5-8; *Poems* (1786), ll. 13-16.

30. "Philip Freneau as Archetypal American Poet," *Literature and Ideas in America: Essays in Memory of Harry Hayden Clark* (Athens: Ohio University Press, 1975), p. 12.

31. Herbert M. Morais, *Deism in Eighteenth Century America* (New York: Columbia University Press, 1934), pp. 21-22, discusses American freethinkers who "adopted the cautious procedure of Freneau and Jefferson who, while bitterly castigating the clergy, did not openly reject revealed religion."

32. *Poems* (1786), pp. 133-52; prefatory stanzas.

33. Freneau to A.B., March 14, 1789, in *Prose Works*, p. 479.

34. *Poems* (1786), pp. 86-87, ll. 9-12.

35. *Ibid.*, pp. 169-71, ll. 1-16.

CHAPTER IV

1. *The Columbian Herald* (July 6, 1786), l. 13.

2. *Works* (1788), p. 152.

3. *Poems* (1795), p. 95.

4. Robert D. Arner, "Neoclassicism and Romanticism: A Reading of Freneau's 'The Wild Honey Suckle,'" *Early American Literature* IX (1974), 53-61, interprets the poem's negativeness as part of the speaker's growing awareness of the flower's postlapsarian mutability.

5. *Freeman's Journal* (April 18, 1787), ll. 1-7.

6. *Works* (1788), pp. 163-65, ll. 56-58.

7. Freneau's marginalia in Isaac Watts, *Works*, 6 vols. (London: Jennings & Doddridge, 1753), V, 28. Copy in Rutgers University Library.

8. *Horae Lyricae: Poems chiefly of the Lyric Kind* (New York: Hugh Gaine, 1762), p. 147.

9. *The Columbian Herald* (July 13, 1786), ll. 25-30.

10. *The Man of Feeling: A Novel, . . . with the Sentimental Sailor: A Poem* (Philadelphia: Robert Bell, 1782), pp. 75-76.

11. *Freeman's Journal* (April 11, 1787), ll. 3-7.

12. Besides publishing a number of Brackenridge's anti-Indian diatribes in news-

papers he controlled, Freneau himself wrote at least two anti-Indian poems, "Stanzas to the memory of Robert and William Sevier" (1792) and "Of Thomas Swagum, an Oneida Indian, and a Missionary Parson" (1797).

13. *Freeman's Journal* (June 20, 1787), 11. 25-26.

14. *The American Museum, or Repository of Ancient and Modern Fugitive Pieces, etc., Prose and Poetical*, II (July-December 1787), 515-16, ll. 1-8.

15. Martin E. Itzkowitz, "Freneau's 'Indian Burying Ground' and 'Keats' 'Grecian Urn,'" *Early American Literature* VI (1971), 258-62, underlines the poem's skepticism.

16. *Poems, Written and Published During the American Revolutionary War* (Philadelphia: Lydia R. Bailey, 1809), vol. II, p. 198 *n*.

17. *The City Gazette, or the Daily Advertiser*, Charleston, S.C. (January 30, 1788), ll. 15-16.

18. *Poems* (1795), p. 80.

19. *Works* (1788), p. 2.

20. Carol A. Kyle, "That Poet Freneau: A Study of the Imagistic Success of *The Pictures of Columbus*," *Early American Literature* IX (1974), 62-70, also finds the conflict between fancy and reality central to the poem's meaning.

21. "Lines Written at Port Royal, in the Island of Jamaica," *Works* (1788), pp. 176-79, ll. 83-84.

22. "Robert Slender's Idea of the Human Soul," *Ibid.*, p. 90.

23. "An Oration upon Rum," *Ibid.*, p. 92.

24. "The Inexorable Captain, A Short Story," *Ibid.*, p. 133.

25. Compare *Works* (1788), p. 254, with *The Freeman's Journal* (July 3, 1782).

26. *Works* (1788), pp. 259-60, ll. 29-30.

27. *Ibid.*, pp. 116-17.

28. *Ibid.*, pp. 162-63.

29. "The Minstrel's Complaint," *Poems* (1795), pp. 313-14.

CHAPTER V

1. "The Poetic Courtship of Philip Freneau, The Poet of the Revolution, and Beautiful Eleanor Forman," *Through the Gates of Old Romance* (Philadelphia: J. B. Lippincott, 1903), pp. 121-55. Leary, *That Rascal Freneau*, p. 160, and Marsh, *Freneau*, p. 114, cautiously accept Mills's contention.

2. *The Freeman's Journal* (January 29, 1789), l. 1.

3. See *The Daily Advertiser* (August 25, 1790), ll. 13 and 19; *Poems* (1795), p. 378; and *Poems* (1809), II, 252.

4. Leary, p. 161, *n*. 80.

5. *The Daily Advertiser* (April 15, 1789).

6. *The Freeman's Journal* (July 18, 1787), ll. 27-30.

7. *The Daily Advertiser* (September 7, 1790), l. 36.

8. *The Daily Advertiser* (November 14, 1789), l. 39; *The National Gazette* (January 16, 1792), l. 47; "Hatteras," *Poems* (1795), pp. 308-10, l. 55.

9. Inspection of the *Daily Advertiser* during the period reveals this orientation plainly. Besides its obvious slant toward the shipping industry in its advertisements and announcements, its accounts of shipwrecks and interesting voyages and other

items of maritime interest take up a sizable part of almost every issue. Freneau's relationship with the paper, culminating with his editing of it during much of 1790, almost certainly grew out of his experience and connections in the merchant fleet.

10. *The Daily Advertiser* (May 1, 1790), ll. 1 and 3.

11. "Constantia," *Poems* (1795), pp. 381-82, ll. 13-18.

12. In both collections, however, Freneau spaced the poems in the series at wide and apparently random intervals, as if trying to hide the fact that originally he wrote them as parts of a single poem. Moreover, he omitted "A View of Rhode Island (Extracted from a new Poem, entitled the Rising Empire, not yet published,)" (*The Daily Advertiser*, February 4, 1790), from both editions, making attribution doubtful enough to have kept me from including the poem in this study, even though it is thematically and symbolically consistent with the other seven.

13. *The Daily Advertiser* (March 13, 1790), l. 2.

14. *The Daily Advertiser* (May 10, 1790), l. 12.

15. *The City Gazette* (February 2, 1790), l. 21.

16. Compare *Poems* (1795), p. 376, and *Poems* (1809), II, 238.

17. Compare *Poems* (1795), p. 355, and *Poems* (1809), II, 246.

18. *The Daily Advertiser* (June 11, 1790), l. 7.

19. "To Harriott," (November 30, 1789) and an untitled poem, later named "The Bird at Sea" and "The Wanderer," (December 10, 1789).

20. See Stuart Piggott, *The Druids* (New York: Praeger, 1968), p. 164.

21. William Cowper, *Poems*, 3 vols. (Baltimore: P. H. Nicklin, 1810), II, 265.

22. *An Enquiry into The Patriarchal and Druidical Religions, Temples, etc.* (London: 1754).

CHAPTER VI

1. *The National Gazette* (November 14, 1791), ll. 17-22.

2. *The Time-Piece and Literary Companion* (December 8, 1797); *Poems* (1809), II, 182-83; and *Poems* (1815), II, 81-83.

3. *The New York Weekly Museum* (August 1 and 8, 1801), ll. 7-8.

4. *The City Gazette* (July 2, 1804), ll. 73, 75, and 77.

5. "Stanzas Written at the island of Madeira," *Poems* (1815), I, 171-76, l. 106.

6. *The City Gazette* (July 9, 1804), l. 3.

7. *Poems* (1815), I, 167-68, ll. 7 and 9.

8. *Poems* (1809), I, 262-63, ll. 19-24.

9. *Ibid.*, 264-65, ll. 37-48.

10. *Poems* (1815), I, 28-30, ll. 1-2.

11. *Ibid.*, 105-6, ll. 7-9.

12. "Belief and Unbelief: Humbly Recommended to the Serious Consideration of Creed Makers," *Ibid.*, 119-21, ll. 9-20.

13. *Ibid.*, 94-95, ll. 21-24.

INDEX

Index

191